KNOWLEDGE OF THE HIGHER WORLDS

AND ITS ATTAINMENT

*Rudolf Steiner's Brilliant Prescription for
How We Can Access Our Higher Being and Help the Earth Evolve*

BY ELIZA JOSLIN KENDALL

— BOOK 2 IN THE SIMPLY STEINER™ SERIES —

Knowledge of the Higher World and Its Attainment: Rudolf Steiner's Brilliant Prescription for How We Can Access Our Higher Being and Help the Earth Evolve, by Eliza Joslin Kendall. Book 2 in the Simply Steiner™ series. Copyright © 2022 by Eliza Joslin Kendall. All rights reserved.

This book may not be reproduced in whole or in part, in any form or by any means, electronic or mechanical, including recording, or by any information storage and retrieval system now known or hereafter invented, without written permission of the publisher. Brief excerpts may be quoted, in print or online, for the purpose of book reviews. For permission requests, contact the publisher, below.

Eliza Joslin Kendall
https://capecodspiritualcoach.com/simply-steiner

Book Developer & Editor: Naomi Rose: www.naomirose.net

Book Design, Typesetting, and Cover:
Molly McWilliams, https://www.mdesignsmarketing.com

Knowledge of the Higher World and Its Attainment: Rudolf Steiner's Brilliant Prescription for How We Can Access Our Higher Being and Help the Earth Evolve, by Eliza Joslin Kendall. Book 2 in the Simply Steiner™ Series.

First edition. Published 2022
Printed in the United States of America.

ISBN #: 978-1-7342627-2-8

THE SIMPLY STEINER™ SERIES

The Gospel of St. John: Revisiting the Vision of Rudolf Steiner for the 21st Century—Our Participation in Earth's Evolution as the Planet of Love, by Eliza Joslin Kendall. Book 1 in the Simply Steiner™ Series"

Knowledge of the Higher Worlds and Its Attainment: Rudolf Steiner's Brilliant Prescription for How We Can Access Our Higher Being and Help the Earth Evolve, *by Eliza Joslin Kendall.* Book 2 in the Simply Steiner™ Series"

Affirmation Cards for *Knowledge of the Higher Worlds and Its Attainment*

All items are available from:
https://capecodspiritualcoach.com/simply-steiner/

"Of further importance is what Spiritual Science calls Orientation into the Higher Worlds. In our soul and thought-worlds, feelings and thoughts react upon each other just as physical objects do in our physical worlds. No paths to higher knowledge may be reached unless we guard our thoughts and feelings in just the same way we guard our steps in the physical world.

"If we see a wall before us, we do not attempt to dash right through it, but turn aside. In other words, we guide ourselves by the laws of the physical world. There are such laws, too, for the worlds of our souls and thoughts. They must not come from without but instead must flow out of the lives of our souls."

"If we regulate our inner lives, we shall soon find ourselves becoming rich in feelings and creative thoughts with genuine imagination. In the place of petty emotionalism and unstable flights of thought appear instead emotions and thoughts that are fruitful. When we gain the right position in relation to the things of the spiritual worlds, distinct and definite results come into effect in our favor. Just as our physical forms find their way among physical things, so, too, do the paths that lead us between growth and decay. On the one hand, we follow all processes of growing and flourishing, and on the other, of withering and decaying in ways that are necessary for our own as well as the world's advancement."

—Rudolf Steiner (from Chapter 2, "The Stages of Initiation")

*I would like to dedicate this book and the Simply Steiner™ Series to Ronald James Kendall, Jr. 1957-2020—
my husband, my soul mate, father of my children, and supportive best friend.*

CONTENTS

Foreword by Clare Goodwin 1

Introduction 3

Chapter 1: HOW IS KNOWLEDGE OF THE HIGHER
WORLDS ATTAINED? 7
Developing the Capacity for Knowledge of the
Higher Worlds 7
    Receiving Initiation from Esoteric Teachings 7
    Developing Interest in Esoteric Knowledge for the
    Uninitiated 8
    Methods to Prepare Students 9
    The Path of Veneration 9
    Overcoming Difficulty in Order to Attain Esoteric
    Knowledge 10
    Transforming Our Innermost Self 11
    Reverence Awakens Sympathetic Powers in Our
    Souls 12
    The Value of Daily Contemplation 13
    Fundamental Principles of Spiritual Science 14
Inner Tranquility 14
    Awakening the Higher Being within Us 17
    The Higher Beings within Us Are in a Constant State
    of Development 19
    The Need to Rise to a Completely Different Human
    Level 20
    A World Where Hidden Beings Speak to Us through
    Our Thoughts 20
    Meditation—The Means to Supersensible
    Knowledge 21
    Seeking the Guidance of Knowledgeable Teachers 22
    Knowledge of Reincarnation 22

CHAPTER 2: THE STAGES OF INITIATION..............................25
The Three Stages of Initiation...25
Stage 1: Preparation..26
Allowing Feelings from Impressions
   to Speak to Us 26
   The Dawning of Our Soul-World....................................27
   Using Our Powers of Observation, Not
   Intellectualizing 28
   Orientation into the Higher Worlds................................28
   The World of Sound..29
   Developing How We Listen to Others..............................30
Stage 2: Enlightenment 32
   The First Steps Towards Enlightenment 32
   The Spiritual Apprehension of Color...............................33
   Increasing Our Moral Strength, Inner Purity, and
   Powers of Observation..34
   Control of Our Thoughts and Feelings............................35
   How to Apply the Necessary Devotion and
   Sympathy to Enlightenment..37
   The Creation of New Powers of Perception 38
   Contemplations of Man Himself
   —The Three Golden Rules 42
   How Enlightened Insight May be Achieved 44
   What Would-Be Initiates Need to Bring Along 45
   The Forces at Work and the Cultivation of Courage
   and Fearlessness..46
Stage 3—Initiation..48
   Review of the Trials Toward Enlightenment...................49
   The Water-Trial 53
   The Importance of the Use of Sound Judgment..............54
   Our Ordinary Lives Are our Esoteric trainings 56
   The Air-Trial—Absolute Presence of Mind....................56
   Draught of Forgetfulness into the Secret Knowledge.....57
   Draught of Remembrance into the Secret Knowledge....58
CHAPTER 3: SOME PRACTICAL ASPECTS........................61
The Important Quality of Patience.......................................61

CHAPTER 4: THE CONDITIONS OF ESOTERIC TRAINING
The Seven Conditions towards Higher Knowledge.................71
   1. *Pay heed to the advancement of our bodily and spiritual health* 72
   2. *Feel synchronized in the whole of life*................73
   3. *Realize that our thoughts and feelings are as important for the world as are our actions*................74
   4. *Acquire the conviction that our real beings do not live in our exterior but in our interior*................74
   5. *Be unwavering in carrying out resolutions*................75
   6. *Develop feelings of thankfulness for everything with which we are favored*................75
   7. *Regard life unceasingly in the manner demanded by these conditions*................76

CHAPTER 5: SOME RESULTS OF INITIATION................81
The Need to Study with Full Consciousness................81
The *Chakras*—Spiritual Lotus Flowers................82
   Throat Chakra—The 16-Petal Lotus................84
   The Eight Functions in Which Our Ideas and Conceptions Are Acquired 85
   Heart Chakra – The 12-Petal Lotus 90
   The Six Attributes Required of Us 91
   Solar Plexus Chakra—The 10-Petal Lotus 95
   Sacral Chakra – 6-Petal Lotus 98
   Hearing the Inner Worlds................99
   Reflections of the Great Laws of Cosmic Evolution......102
   We Become Gifted with the Inner Worlds................103
   The Four Attributes Must Be Incorporated into our Souls 104
   The Founders/Initiates of the Great Cosmogonies........106
   Spiritual Figures and the Throat Chakra—16-Petal Lotus ...107
   Inner Perception 109
   The Significance of Our Third-Eye Lotus (Chakra) 111
   Our Higher Selves................111

CHAPTER 6: THE TRANSFORMATION OF DREAM LIFE.115
Knowledge of Our Higher Self and Higher Consciousness..118

CHAPTER 7: THE CONTINUITY OF CONSCIOUSNESS ...123
Deep Sleep..124

CHAPTER 8: THE SPLITTING OF THE HUMAN
PERSONALITY DURING SPIRITUAL TRAINING................131
The Dangers Concerning Ascension into the Higher
Worlds..132
The Spiritual Worlds Define the Facts of Our Physical World..........133
Development of Fundamental Forces of our Souls: Willing,
Feeling, Thinking..134
The Thought-Brain, the Feeling-Brain, and the Will-Brain....135
Three Deviations that May Occur..137

CHAPTER 9: THE GUARDIAN OF THE THRESHOLD........141

CHAPTER 10: LIFE AND DEATH: THE GREATER
GUARDIAN OF THE THRESHOLD..149
The Second, Greater Guardian of the Threshold....................153

APPENDIX TO STEINER'S LATEST EDITION (1918)...........157
ACKNOWLEDGMENTS..161
ABOUT THE AUTHOR 162
TO GO FURTHER 164

FOREWORD

Rudolph Steiner's writings were first introduced to me by my astrology and tarot teacher in 1979. At the time, I was a single mother of two small children. Exhausted, as I attempted to read his books the words quickly became a blur and I would fall asleep. Eventually, I gave up on trying to understand and let it go. Steiner was clearly for people with more intellectual comprehension than I could muster back then.

When I began to pursue my own artistic and counseling practice, the philosophy of Carl Jung, noted Swiss psychiatrist, informed my vocation of creating mandalas while becoming an intuitive therapist. Roberto Assagioli, an Italian contemporary of Jung and founder of the transpersonal therapy Psychosynthesis, spoke to my spirit and brought a psychological foundation to my intuitive knowing.

In 2011, when Eliza first contacted me for counseling, she tentatively said, "You will think this is weird, but a bird tapped on my window and I clearly heard the words: "Call Clare Goodwin."' Truthfully, I did not think it was strange at all. It was impressive that Eliza had such a strong relationship with the spirit world.

As we worked together, she began to share stories of how spirits would come to her. Eliza quickly learned to set boundaries in both the physical and in the metaphysical world. After a time, I asked her what she read for spiritual inspiration. Imagine my surprise when she immediately responded: "Rudolf Steiner!" Subsequently, she followed her intuitive skill and soul's calling to write not one but two books on his work. Knowing Eliza Kendall, I suspect this is only the beginning.

If you have had "You will think this is weird...." experiences and want to know how to deepen your connection with the spirit world, *Knowledge of the Higher Worlds and Its Attainment* will offer you clear guidance and practical steps for how to achieve that. If you are a seasoned practitioner, this book will give you a 21st-century, easily understood foundation in Steiner's groundbreaking work.

May you and yours receive infinite Divine blessings.

Clare Goodwin
Intuitive Guide and Counselor
Cape Cod, MA
Author, *Gifts of the Mandala: A Guided Journey of Self-Discovery and The Mandala Deck Oracle Cards*

INTRODUCTION

"There slumbers in all human beings the means to acquire the knowledge of the higher worlds."
—Rudolf Steiner

Close to ten years ago, when I was in my mid-50s, I finally decided to complete my bachelor's degree. A few short years later, I became certified in mediation, esoteric healing, and transformational life coaching. But although I accomplished a lot in a short period of time and began receiving and enjoying my new clients, I was clearly getting another, deeper soulful calling. Intuitively, I reached for one of my many Steiner books from one of my many bookshelves and started reading. And there it began.

My life started taking on a whole new meaning. Steiner's writings, which I had been familiar with for many years, now affected me on a deeper, more soulful level than ever before. I felt compelled to bring his philosophies and visions to people in *our time*—to the 21st century. And so, in early 2019, I decided to publish the "Simply Steiner"© series.

Rudolf Steiner (1861-1925)—a visionary dedicated to finding a synthesis between science and spirituality—initially gained recognition in the late 19th century. He had many followers, but his writing is not inherently easy to decipher; many people believe that Steiner intentionally wrote/spoke in a difficult manner to make readers think more deeply. But while it is true that he did indeed want readers to think, he also wanted people to be able to comprehend the contents at a soulful level, rather than just at the level of the words.

My concept of the "Simply Steiner"© series was to offer a more simplified version of Steiner's thoughts, books, and lectures, but to keep the content fully intact. The first book in this series, *The Gospel of St. John: Revisiting the Vision of Rudolf Steiner for the 21st Century*, was written in the Spring of 2019 and published in February 2020. This book that you are holding now, *Knowledge of the Higher Worlds and Its Attainment*, is the second in the series. Because this book is so densely rich with Steiner's spiritual gems that need to be contemplated and made personally relevant, I also developed a set of Affirmation cards, with quotes correlated with the chapters, to be used for book club material or as a Select-from-the-Deck affirmations by readers and for practitioner use as well.

At the time that I was writing *Knowledge of the Higher Worlds* in 2019, I knew that it was my calling and something that needed to be written, read, and discussed. I knew that a growing number of people would be interested in Steiner, especially at this time in our history and human evolution. But I had no idea of the huge changes soon to come that would affect all our lives, and my life in particular: I had no idea that in 2020 there would be a worldwide pandemic, nor that my husband/best friend/life partner would pass of cancer in August of 2020, and that my life as I once knew it would completely change.

Even as a small child, I have always felt I had a choir of persons looking over me. My connections with those who have passed and with the higher worlds grows ever deeper. Now, my husband sits among the growing group. I continue to believe that bringing Steiner and his philosophy to the public is greatly needed, especially in today's world, and that together you and I may collectively bring forth more loving and positive changes that the world deeply needs, and that Steiner actually foretold.

"If we do not develop within ourselves this deeply rooted feeling that there is something higher than ourselves, we shall never find the strength to evolve to something higher."

—Rudolf Steiner

ABOUT RUDOLF STEINER

Rudolf Steiner, born in Austria (February 1861-March 30, 1925), initially gained recognition at the end of the 19th century as a literary critic and an author of philosophical works, including the *Philosophy of Freedom*. But it is his later contributions that tend to persist into our own time. At the beginning of the 20th century, he founded an esoteric spiritual movement known as anthroposophy (with roots in German idealistic philosophy and theosophy, as well as the thinking of Goethe and Rosicrucianism), which is still vital today. He came up with the Waldorf approach to education, which still thrives internationally as Waldorf Schools. In addition, he is responsible for biodynamic agriculture, so relevant to our own era's need to heal the human relationship to nature. He made many other unique contributions to the realms of thought, spiritual life, and the embodiment of spiritual life, as well.

Dedicated to finding a synthesis between science and spirituality, Steiner came up with what he came to call "Spiritual Science," a philosophy that applied the clarity of Western philosophy to spiritual questions. He first began speaking publicly about spiritual experiences and phenomena in his lectures to the Theosophical Society. By 1901, he had begun to write about spiritual topics. By 1904, he was expressing his own understanding of these themes in his essays and books.

"A world of spiritual perception is discussed in a number of writings which I have published," he wrote. "*The Philosophy of Freedom* . . . tries to show that the experience of thinking, rightly understood, is in fact an experience of spirit."

Applying his training in mathematics, science, and philosophy to produce rigorous, verifiable presentations of spiritual experiences, he believed that anyone—through ethical disciplines and meditative training—could develop the ability to experience the spiritual worlds, including the higher nature of oneself and others, and thereby become capable of actions motivated solely by love.

Steiner's works confronted many conventional categories

and encompassed numerous disciplines and specialties. He was a philosopher, a theologian, an educator, an architectural expert, an architect, an expert in medicinal plants, a dramatist, an authority on Goethe, a clairvoyant and esotericist, a social reformer, an economist, and an artistic trendsetter. In short, he was a creative genius. Steiner had supersensible perception starting at a very young age, and as an adult he aimed to find scientific methods for developing and cultivating those powers within ourselves by means of our conscious and deliberate thoughts. He believed that divine creativity is not simply a repetition of something already existing, but that the mission of the earth is the cultivation of the principle of love to its highest degree by those beings involved in evolving upon it. When the earth has reached the end of its evolution, love will pervade it through and through. These tasks became his life's work.

It is my hope that in reading this book, you will be introduced to areas of your own spiritual nature that you may not be familiar with, or at least not in the ways Steiner presents them. You will encounter the need for reverence (Chapter 1), the stages of initiation, including secret knowledge (Chapter 2), the importance of patience and other practical considerations (Chapter 3), the seven conditions of esoteric training (Chapter 4), the chakras (Chapter 5), the transformation of dream life (Chapter 6), the continuity of consciousness (Chapter 7), the splitting of the human personality during training (Chapter 8), and the Guardians of the Threshold (Chapters 9 and 10).

Be of good courage, as you read; don't be dissuaded by the challenges Steiner presents. The person you may become by giving yourself to the contents of this book may well be the person you deeply, spiritually long to be. And that person will have the clarity, intelligence, heart, and power to help the earth evolve into what Steiner has prophesied in *The Gospel of St. John* and other places: the planet of love.

– Chapter 1 –

How Is Knowledge of the Higher Worlds Attained

Developing the Capacity for Knowledge of the Higher Worlds

There slumbers in all human beings the means to acquire the knowledge of the higher worlds. Mystics, theosophists, Gnostics—all speak of a world of souls and spirits that, for them, is just as real as the world we see with our physical eyes or touch with our physical hands. At every moment we may say to ourselves that what they speak of, we can learn too, if we develop within ourselves certain powers that slumber within us. There remains only one question—how to set to work the development of such faculties/abilities.

Receiving Initiation from Esoteric Teachings

For these purposes, those that may offer advice already possess these powers. **As long as human beings have existed, there has always been a method of training those in search of these higher facilities by individuals possessing them. Such trainings are called occult (esoteric) trainings, and the instructions received from them are called esoteric teachings, or Spiritual Science.**

This description may awaken misunderstanding. Those who hear this term may easily be misled to believe that this training is only of concern to a special or privileged class, and therefore that this knowledge is not readily available to fellow human beings. They might ask themselves, "If this is true knowledge, there should be no need of making it secret; it should be publicly conveyed and their advantages made accessible to all."

However, those who have been initiated into the nature of this higher knowledge are not in the least surprised that the uninitiated should think this way, for the secrets of initiation can only be understood by those who have, to a certain degree, experienced initiation into the higher knowledge of existence.

Developing Interest in Esoteric Knowledge for the Uninitiated

The question may then be raised: "How are the uninitiated to develop any human interest in this so-called esoteric knowledge? How and why would someone want to seek knowledge for something about which they do not yet form any idea or comprehend?" The truth is, there is no difference between esoteric knowledge, and all the rest of man's knowledge and proficiency. Esoteric knowledge is no more of a secret than our learning to read and write. And just as those who learned to read and write did so by choosing the right methods, so too may all those who seek the right way become esoteric students, and even become teachers. *There are no obstacles for those who earnestly seek it.*

Many believe that they must first seek the masters of higher knowledge in order that they may receive enlightenment, and they fiercely search for initiates who may lead them to higher knowledge of the world. Everyone may rest assured that in all circumstances the initiates will find them, if they earnestly strive to attain this knowledge.

It is natural law among all initiates/teachers to not withhold knowledge from those who are qualified to learn it; but there is an equally natural law that esoteric knowledge shall not be imparted to anyone not qualified to receive it. The bond and union embracing all initiates is spiritual, not external. What is most important is that we are able, at the present stage of evolution, to receive it into our souls in the correct manner.

Methods to Prepare Students

The methods by which students are prepared for the reception of higher knowledge is clearly prescribed. These directions can be traced back to unfading, everlasting letters in the world of spirit where the initiates guard these secrets. In ancient times, the temples of the spirit were outwardly visible; today, because our lives have become less spiritual (and more materialistic), they are not to be found in our visible sights. Yet they are present spiritually everywhere, and all that seek them will find them.

The Path of Veneration

Only within our own souls may we find the means to unseal the lips of the initiates. But first we must develop within ourselves certain capacities, for only then the highest treasures of the spirit may become our own. We must begin with certain fundamental attitudes of our souls. In Spiritual Science, these paths are called *the paths of veneration* (respect, devotion, and knowledge). Without these attitudes, no one may become a student. These dispositions—shown at the time of childhood by subsequent students of higher knowledge—are well known to those who are experienced in these matters. Such children grow up into young men and women who feel happy when they can look up to anything that fills them with *veneration*. From the ranks of such children are recruited many students of higher knowledge. Experience teaches that those who can best hold their heads high are those who have learned to *venerate* when *veneration* is due, and this is always fitting when it flows from the depths of our hearts.

If we do not develop within ourselves this deeply rooted feeling that there is something higher than ourselves, we shall never find the strength to evolve to something higher. The initiates have only to develop these strengths to lift their heads to the heights, to the depths, of their *veneration* (respect, admiration, and devotion). The heights of the spirit can only be climbed by passing the portals of humility. We may only acquire right knowledge when we have learned to esteem it. We certainly *have* the right to turn our eyes towards these lights, but we must first *acquire* these rights.

There are laws in the spiritual life, as in the physical life. Rub a glass rod with an appropriate material and it will become electrical (static electricity) — that is, it will receive the power of attraction. This is in keeping with the laws of nature. Similarly, acquaintance with the first principles of Spiritual Science shows that every feeling of true devotion harbored within our souls develops powers which may, sooner or later, lead us further on these paths of knowledge.

Overcoming Difficulty in Order to Attain Esoteric Knowledge

What must be acknowledged are the difficulties for those involved in the external civilizations of our times in attaining the knowledge of the higher worlds. We can only do so if we are determined to do so. At a time when the conditions of our material lives were simpler, the attainment of spiritual knowledge was easier. Objects of veneration and worship stood out clearly to offer assistance and reassurance from the ordinary things in the world. In our epoch of criticism, ideals are/were lowered, and other feelings have taken the place of these venerations. Our own age thrusts these feelings further and further into the background, so that they can only be conveyed to us in our everyday lives to a small degree.

*"Whoever seeks higher knowledge must
create and then instill it into their soul.
It cannot be done by study; it can only be done through life.
Therefore, whoever wishes to seek higher knowledge
must diligently and earnestly cultivate
their inner lives of devotion."*

Everywhere in our environments and in our experiences, we must seek motives of admiration and homage. If, when we meet another, we remind them of their shortcomings, we are robbing ourselves of these powers to attain higher knowledge; but if we try to enter lovingly and with integrity, we will gather such powers. We must continually be intent upon following this advice.

Transforming Our Innermost Self

*"We have in us the power to perfect ourselves,
and in time, completely transform ourselves.
But these transformations must take place
in our innermost selves, in our inner thought-lives."*

It is not enough that we show respect only in our outward attitudes and behaviors, but we must also absorb these devotions into our inner thoughts. We must be wary of thoughts of disrespect, and of negative criticisms existing in our consciousness, and must instead aim to instantaneously cultivate thoughts of devotion.

In these ways, our spiritual eyes are opened, which otherwise would have remained dormant. We begin to see things around us that we had never seen before. We begin to understand and realize that we had only been seeing a part of the world that surrounds us. A human being standing before us now presents in a wholly different aspect.

*"Every moment that we set ourselves to discover and
remove that which remains in our consciousness
that are adverse, disparaging, or critical judgments of the
world and of life brings us nearer to this higher knowledge."*

Noiseless and unnoticed by the outer worlds are the treadings of the *Paths of Knowledge*. No changes in us will be noticed by others. All our duties are performed, and all our businesses are attended to, per usual. These transformations go only in the inner parts of our souls, hidden from outward sight.

At first our inner lives are flooded by feelings of devotion for everything which is truly sacred. Our entire soul-lives find in these fundamental feelings their centers. Just as the sun's rays invigorate everything that is living, so does this reverence in us invigorate all our feelings in our souls.

> *"It is not easy, at first,*
> *to believe that these feelings of reverence*
> *and respect would have anything to do with*
> *our cognitions (reasoning, comprehension, and insight).*
> *This is due to the fact that we are inclined to set our*
> *cognitions aside as capacities in and of themselves, and as*
> *if they have no relationship to what occurs in our <u>souls</u>.*
> *In so thinking, we do not bear in mind that it is our souls*
> *which exercise our capacities of cognition;*
> *feelings are, for our souls, what food is to our bodies."*

Veneration, homage, respect, and devotion are like nutriments, and are the making of healthy and strong (especially strong) activities of our cognition. Our disrespect, antipathy, and underestimation of what deserve our recognitions all exert paralyzing and withering effects on the faculties of our cognitions.

Reverence Awakens Sympathetic Powers in Our Souls

> *"Reverence awakens in our souls as sympathetic powers,*
> *through which we attract the qualities in those beings around*
> *us, which would otherwise have remained concealed."*

These powers, obtained through our devotion, are rendered even more effective when the lives of our feelings are enriched by another quality: giving ourselves less to our impressions of the outer worlds, and developing more meaningful inner lives instead.

Those who dart from one impression of the outer worlds to another, and who are constantly seeking distractions, cannot find their way to this higher knowledge. However, we must not dull ourselves from the outer worlds and their impressions, but instead lend ourselves to these impressions and direct them to our own rich inner lives.

For example: Travelers who pass through beautiful mountain scenes with the depths of their souls and the wealth of their feelings have different experiences from those who are poor in these feelings. **Only what we experience within ourselves unlocks for us the beauties of the outer worlds.** We must learn to remain in touch with our own feelings and ideas, if we wish to develop these intimate relationships with the outer worlds. The outer worlds, with all their phenomena, are filled with divine splendors; but we must have first experienced the divine within ourselves before we can hope to discover it in our environments.

The Value of Daily Contemplation

We need to set apart moments in our daily lives in which to withdraw inwardly, quietly, and alone. At these moments, we are not to occupy ourselves with the affairs of our own egos. We should let our experiences and messages from the outer worlds re-echo within our completely silent selves. In these silent moments, every flower, every animal, every action will unveil to us secrets we have never dreamed of. We are now prepared to receive quite new impressions of the outer worlds through our quite different eyes. These impressions are nurtured and cultivated if the enjoyment that is being experienced can reveal their message(s).

We must now accustom ourselves to work upon the experiences themselves. The peril, here, is very great. Instead of working inwardly, it is extremely easy to fall into the opposite habit: of trying to experience and exploit the enjoyment. **Seekers of higher knowledge must consider this enjoyment only as** a means of enthroning ourselves for the world. We should not learn to accumulate this learning as our own treasure, but only in order that we may devote this learning to the service of the world.

Fundamental Principles of Spiritual Science

In all Spiritual Science, there are fundamental principles which cannot be broken without sacrificing our success; and this should be impressed upon in all forms of our esoteric training.

It is as follows: All knowledge that is pursued merely for the enrichment of personal learning and the accumulation of personal treasure leads us away from the path; but all knowledge pursued from growth to maturity within these processes of human ennoblement and cosmic developments brings us steps forward.

These laws must be strictly observed, and we are not genuine until we have adopted them as our guide for our entire lives. These truths can be expressed by the following sentence: Every idea which does not become your ideal slays a force in your soul; every idea which becomes your ideal creates within yourself life-forces.

Inner Tranquility

At the very beginning of this book, we were directed to the paths of veneration (devotion) and the development of our inner lives. **Spiritual Science now also gives us practical rules for observing which paths to follow to develop our inner lives.**
The practical rules have no arbitrary origins. They rest upon ancient experiences and ancient wisdoms, and are given out in the same manner. All true teachers of the spiritual life agree as to the substance of these rules, even though they do not always phrase them in the same words.

No teachers of the spiritual life wish to establish mastery over any other person by means of such rules. They will not tamper with anyone's independence. Indeed, no one respects and cherishes human independence more than the spiritually experienced. It was stated in the preceding pages that the bonds and unions embracing all those seeking this higher knowledge are spiritual, and that there are two laws formed by which the component parts of these bonds are held together.

Whenever we leave our enclosed spiritual spheres and step forth before the world, we must immediately take another law into account. It is this: **We must adapt each one of our actions and frame each one of our words in such a way that we infringe upon no one else's free-will.**

One of the first of these rules may be expressed in the following words:

All those who seek the knowledge of the higher worlds must provide for themselves moments of inner tranquility, and in these moments learn to distinguish between the essential and the non-essential.

Originally, all rules and teachings of Spiritual Science were expressed in a symbolical sign-language, of which some understanding must be acquired before their whole meaning and scope could be realized. These understandings are dependent on our first steps toward higher knowledge, and these steps result from our exact observations of such rules given. For all of us who earnestly will embark on such a path, the paths stand open for us to walk. But they only may be achieved when observed earnestly and through extremely strict manners, even though in and of themselves they appear quite simple.

15

Setting Aside Daily Time to Move Beyond Our Usual Self-Perception

We must set aside small parts of our daily lives in which to concern ourselves with something quite different from the objects of our own daily lives. But this does not mean that what we do during these times is to be set apart from, and has no connection with, our daily tasks. On the contrary, we will soon find that these secluded moments, when sought in the right ways, give fuller powers to perform these daily tasks. Nor must the observance of these rules encroach upon the times needed for the performance of our duties. *If anyone should really have no more time at their disposal, five minutes a day will be fine. It all depends on the way these five minutes are spent.*

During these periods, we should rest ourselves and be entirely free from distractions. Our thoughts and feelings should take on different complexions. All our joys and sorrows, cares, experiences, and actions must pass in review before our souls; and we must adopt positions to regard all our various experiences from higher points of view.

Now we also need to bear in mind how, in our ordinary lives, we regard the experiences and actions of others quite differently from those of our own. This is because we are interwoven with our own actions and experiences, whereas those of others we only consider. *Our aims in these moments of seclusion must be to contemplate and judge our own actions and experiences as though they were applied not to us personally but to some other person (thinking outside of ourselves).*

For example: If a misfortune hits us and the same misfortune hits our neighbors, would our attitudes toward these misfortunes be the same? These attitudes cannot be blamed as unjustified, as it is only part of our human natures, and it applies equally to exceptional circumstances as it does to our everyday lives.

If our experiences are interwoven, we cling to the non-important just as much as we do to the important. However, if we attain calm inner surveys, those matters which are important are severed from those which are unimportant. Our sorrows, our joys, all our thoughts, all our resolves appear different when we confront ourselves in these ways. It is as though we had spent our entire days in places where we beheld the smallest objects at the same close range as the largest, and in the evenings climbed neighboring hills and surveyed the entire scene at a glance. We find that these various parts now relate to each other in quite different proportions from when we viewed them from within.

"We must seek the power of confronting ourselves, at certain times, as complete and total strangers. We must stand before ourselves with the inner tranquility of a judge. When this is attained, all our experiences present themselves in new lights."

These exercises need not be limited only to our present circumstances, but they also should be attempted in connection with our past circumstances. *The value of these inner tranquil self-contemplations depends far less on what is contemplated than on our finding within us the powers where such inner tranquilities develop.*

Awakening the Higher Being within Us

"Every human being bears higher beings that lie within, which remain hidden until awakened. We, as individuals, are the only ones who can awaken these higher beings concealed within us."

If our higher beings are not awakened, these higher powers that lead to supersensible knowledge will remain concealed. *To those who resolve to persevere on these roads to higher knowledge, the day will come when spiritual lights will envelop them and new worlds will be revealed within.*

No outward changes need take place. Little by little, our higher lives will engage in our ordinary lives. Our entire being will grow calmer, and we will attain firm assurances in all our actions. By advancing in these matters, we will gradually become more and more our own guides, allowing ourselves to be led less by circumstances and external influences.

We will soon discover that great sources of strength are available to us. We will begin to no longer get angry at things that formerly would have annoyed us, as we now will have developed entirely new outlooks on our lives. Formerly we may have approached some situations in fearful ways. We may have said: "Oh, I lack the power to do this." Now, these thoughts do not even occur to us. Now, we may say to ourselves: "I will summon all my strength to do this as well as I possibly can."

We are now able to suppress those thoughts which made us fearful. We now realize that those very thoughts may have caused substandard performances on our parts, and they certainly did not contribute to any improvements in our work. We now have a better outlook on our lives, and this new outlook now takes the place of those old outlooks that had hampering, weakening effects. *We now begin to steer our own ships on secure courses through the waves of our lives, whereas formerly we were battered to and fro by these waves. Now, a greater sense of calm and serenity respond to our entire beings (selves). Within our inner beings (selves), these greater capacities lead us to higher knowledge.*

If we continue to proceed in this direction, we will gradually reach the point where we ourselves determine the manner in which the impressions of the outer worlds shall affect us. We may hear words spoken with the objectives of wounding or hurting us. Formerly, these words may have wounded or hurt us, but now that we tread the path to higher knowledge, we are able to take away the stings and the powers to wound or vex us. Another example: At one time we may have become easily impatient when we were kept waiting, but now the impatience that was about to make itself known vanishes, and intervals which would otherwise have been wasted in expressions of our impatience are now filled by our useful observations.

THE HIGHER BEINGS WITHIN US ARE IN A CONSTANT STATE OF DEVELOPMENT

The scope and significance of this fact is of extreme importance. We must bear in mind that the higher beings within us are in a constant state of development.

"No outward forces can supply space to our inner selves. They are only supplied by the inner calm which we ourselves give to our souls. Outward circumstances can only alter the courses of our outward lives; they can never awaken our inner spiritual selves."

Our higher inner beings (selves) have now become our rulers, and it is they that direct and guide the circumstances of our outer beings (selves). As long our outer being (selves) have the upper hand and control, our inner beings (selves) are enslaved. We must develop the ability of letting these impressions of the outer world approach us only in ways in which we ourselves determine. We must earnestly seek these powers to reach our goals.

It is not of any importance how far or fast we are going at any given time; the point is that we should earnestly seek these powers out. Many have strived for years without noticing any appreciable progress; and many of the same who have also held their resolve, and did not despair and remained unshaken, have then quickly and suddenly achieved their inner victories.

There is no doubt that great effort is required in many situations to provide moments of inner calm; but the greater the effort, the more valuable the achievement. In Spiritual Science, everything depends upon our energy, inward truthfulness, and uncompromising sincerity with which we confront our own selves with all of our own deeds and actions, as if we were complete strangers looking outside from within.

The Need to Rise to a Completely Different Human Level

Only one side of our inner activities is characterized by the birth of our own higher beings. Something else is needed: **We must now disengage ourselves and rise beyond to a completely different human level.** We must now contemplate and concern ourselves as if we lived under quite different circumstances and involve ourselves in quite different situations.

In this way, something begins to live within ourselves which ranges above the purely personal. Our gaze is directed to worlds higher than those encompassed by our every-day lives. We now begin to feel and realize, as our own inner experiences, that we belong to these higher worlds.

We now shift the central point of our being into the inner part of our natures. We listen to the voice within ourselves which speaks to us in those moments of tranquility, cultivating our inter-relationships with the spiritual worlds. We are removed from our every-day worlds. Their noises are silenced. We put aside everything that reminds us of any impressions from without us. We now, with inward calm, contemplate and converse with the purely spiritual worlds. They fill our souls.

A World Where Hidden Beings Speak to Us through Our Thoughts

Such tranquil contemplations must become natural necessities in our lives. *We are now plunged into worlds of thoughts. We must develop living feelings for these silent thought-activities. We must learn to love what the spirit pours into us.*

We will soon cease to feel that these thought-worlds are any less real than the every-day things which surround us. We discover that something living expresses itself in our thought-worlds. **We find that our thoughts do not merely harbor shadow-pictures, but that through them, hidden beings speak to us.**

Out of the silence, speech becomes audible to us. Formerly, sound only reached us through our ears; now it resounds through our souls. An inner language, an inner word is revealed. These moments, when first experienced, are one of greatest raptures. Inner light is shed over the whole external world, and a second life begins for us. Through our beings pours a divine stream from a world of divine rapture.

Meditation
The Means to Supersensible Knowledge

The lives of our souls in our thoughts, which gradually widen into lives in our spiritual beings, are called—by Gnosis and by Spiritual Science—Meditation (*contemplative reflection*). *Meditation is the* **means to supersensible knowledge.** In these moments, we must not merely indulge in our feelings, for this will only hinder our reaching true spiritual knowledge. We must not cling blindly to the thoughts that rise within us. We must permeate ourselves with the lofty thoughts by which those who are already advanced and possessed of the spirit have been inspired.

We must start with the writings themselves, with their origins and the introductions to these revelations, during our meditations. *In mystic, Gnostic, and spiritual scientific literatures of today, there may be found such writings, and in them the materials for these meditations. These seekers of the spirit have themselves set down in such writings the thoughts of the divine sciences which the Spirit has directed its messengers to proclaim to the world.*

"Through meditation, complete transformations take place. We begin to form quite new conceptions of our realities. All things acquire fresh and new values."

It cannot be repeated too often that these transformations will not, and do not, alienate us from the outside world. We will in no way be estranged from our daily tasks and duties, for we have now come to realize that even the most mundane of actions that must be performed, and the most insignificant experiences that must be attended, all stand in connection with cosmic beings and cosmic events.

Once these connections have been revealed to us in our moments of contemplation, our daily activities come before us with new and fuller powers. *For now, we know that all our labors and our sufferings are given and endured for the sake of a greater, spiritual, cosmic whole.* With firm steps, we will pass through our lives. No matter what our lives may bring before us, we move forward erect. In the past we did not know why we labored and suffered, but now we know.

Seeking the Guidance of Knowledgeable Teachers

It is indisputable that meditation leads more surely to these goals; but it must be conducted under the direction of experienced persons who know, themselves, how everything is best done; their advice and guidance should always be sought. What would otherwise be mere uncertain groping in the dark becomes, under such direction, purposeful work.

It is important that we realize that what we seek is the advice of well-wishers, not the domination of would-be rulers. It will always be found that those who really know are the most modest of people, and that nothing is further from their nature than what is called the lust for power.

When, by means of meditation, we rise to union with the spirit, we bring to our lives the eternal beings, which are limited by neither birth nor death. The existence of these eternal beings can only be doubted by those who have not, themselves, experienced them. Thus meditation is the way which also leads us to this knowledge, to the contemplation of our eternal, indestructible, essential beings; and it is only through meditation that we may attain such knowledge.

Knowledge of Reincarnation

Gnosis and Spiritual Science speak of our eternal nature and of reincarnation. A question often raised is: "Why do we know nothing of our experiences beyond the borders of our lives and deaths?" What should be asked instead is: "How can we attain such knowledge?" In the right meditations, the paths are opened. These alone can revive the memories of experiences beyond the borders of our lives and our deaths.

Everyone can attain this knowledge; in each one of us lies the ability of recognizing and contemplating for ourselves what genuine Mysticism, Spiritual Science, Anthroposophy, and Gnosis teach. Only, the right means must be chosen. Spiritual Science gives these means of developing the spiritual ears and eyes, and of kindling the spiritual lights; and these methods of spiritual training.

– Chapter 2 –

THE STAGES OF INITIATION

The information given in the following chapter constitutes steps in esoteric training. It refers to the three stages through which the training of our spiritual lives leads to a certain degree of initiation. Certain exercises enable our souls to attain conscious communication with the spiritual worlds. The exercises offered bear about the same relation as the instruction given in higher, strictly disciplined schools in basic trainings. Any impatient dabbling, devoid of earnest perseverance, will lead us to nothing at all. These studies of Spiritual Science can only be successful if students have retained what has already been foretold in the previous chapters.

The Three Stages of Initiation

The three stages through which the training of our spiritual lives lead to certain degree of initiation are as follows: **(1)** *Preparation;* **(2)** *Enlightenment;* **(3)** *Initiation.*

It is not altogether necessary that the first of these three stages should be completed before the second can be begun, nor that the second, in turn, be completed before the third is started. In a certain respect, it is possible to partake of enlightenment and even of initiation, and in another respect still be in the preparatory stages.

Yet it will be necessary to spend a certain time in the stage of preparation before any enlightenment can begin; and, at least in some respect, enlightenment must be completed before it is even possible to enter upon the stage of initiation.

But in describing them, it is necessary, for the sake of clarity, that the three stages are placed in the following order.

Stage 1: Preparation

Preparation consists of strict and definite knowledge concerning the life of our thoughts and feelings with our higher senses and organs of activity, in the same way that natural forces have fitted our physical bodies.

We start by bringing our attention to events in the world which surrounds us. On the one hand, we find life that is budding, growing, and flourishing; and on the other hand, we also find all the same phenomena connected with fading, decaying, and withering. We observe these events simultaneously wherever we turn our eyes, and they naturally call forth in us thoughts and feelings.

On ordinary occasions we do not devote sufficient time to these thoughts and feelings. We hurry on too quickly from one impression to another impression. It is necessary, therefore, that we should fix our attentions intently and consciously upon these wonders. Wherever we observe definite kinds of blooming and flourishing, we must banish everything else from our souls, and entirely surrender ourselves, for short times, to these impressions. We shall soon find that feelings which, at similar times, would merely have skimmed through our souls have now become heightened, and assume more powerful and energetic forms.

Allowing Feelings from Impressions to Speak to Us

We must now allow these feelings to rebound quietly within ourselves while keeping inwardly still. We must cut ourselves off from the outer world, and simply allow our souls to speak to us.

First, we must look at these things as keenly and as intently as we possibly can; and then let our feelings expand, arise, and take possession of our souls. Our attention should be directed towards perfect inner balance upon both phenomena. If tranquility is achieved and we surrender ourselves to these feelings, they expand to life in our souls; and in due time, the following experiences will come about.

Many thoughts and feelings of new kinds, unknown before, will be noticed uprising in our souls. The more often that we fix our attention alternately upon something growing, blooming, and flourishing, and then upon something else that is fading and decaying, the more vivid these feelings become. And just as the eyes and ears of our physical bodies are built by natural forces out of living matter, so will our organs of clairvoyance build themselves out of the feelings and thoughts awakened by these. Quite definite forms of feelings connect with growth and expansion, and other equally definite forms of feelings connect with those which are fading and decaying.

Once we start placing more of our attention on the phenomena of growing, blooming, and flourishing, feelings remotely allied to the sensation of the sun rising will ensue; while the phenomena of fading and decaying will produce in us experiences comparable, in the same way, to the slow rising of the moon on the horizon. Both these feelings are forces which, when cultivated and developed to ever increasing intensity, lead us to the most significant of spiritual results. New worlds will be opened to us if we systematically and deliberately surrender ourselves to such feelings.

The Dawning of Our Soul-Worlds

Our soul-worlds, or what are also called our astral planes, will begin to dawn upon us. Now, growth and decay are no longer facts beyond our comprehension; they form themselves into spiritual lines and figures. Those of blooming flowers, animals in the process of growth, and trees that are decaying evoke in our souls different lines. We see and feel with deeper clarity. Our soul worlds (astral planes) will broaden out slowly before us.

These lines and figures are in no sense random. Once we have reached this corresponding stage of development, we will always see the same lines and figures under the same conditions. And just as the forms of animals and plants are described in ordinary natural history, so too, the spiritual scientist describes or draws the spiritual forms of the processes of growth and decay, according to species and kinds.

USING OUR POWERS OF OBSERVATION, NOT INTELLECTUALIZING

Having progressed thus far, it now must be emphasized that we must never lose ourselves speculating the meanings of any one thing or another. Such intellectualizing will only draw us away from the correct road. We should look out on the world with keen, healthy senses and quickened powers of observation. Once there, we need to let these feelings arise within us and allow these things to disclose themselves. **It should be noted that artistic feelings, when coupled with the silent introspection of nature, form the best preliminary conditions for the development of spiritual propensity.** These feelings pierce through the superficial aspects of things, and in doing so touch on their secrets.

ORIENTATION INTO THE HIGHER WORLDS

"Of further importance is what Spiritual Science calls Orientation into the Higher Worlds. In our soul and thought-worlds, feelings and thoughts react upon each other just as physical objects do in our physical worlds."

No paths to higher knowledge may be reached unless we guard our thoughts and feelings in just the same way we guard our steps in the physical world. If we see a wall before us, we do not attempt to dash right through it, but turn aside. In other words, we guide ourselves by the laws of the physical world. **There are such laws, too, for the worlds of our souls and thoughts. They must not come from without but instead must flow out of the lives of our souls.**

If we regulate our inner lives, we shall soon find ourselves becoming rich in feelings and creative thoughts with genuine imagination. In the place of petty emotionalism and unstable flights of thought appear instead emotions and thoughts that are fruitful. When we gain the right position in relation to the things of the spiritual worlds, distinct and definite results come into effect in our favor. Just as our physical forms find their way among physical things, so, too, do the paths that lead us between growth and decay, as described above. On the one hand, we follow all processes of growing and flourishing, and on the other, of withering and decaying in ways that are necessary for our own as well as the world's advancement.

The World of Sound

We must now commit further care to the world of sound. We must be able to discriminate between the sound that is produced by an inert or lifeless body—for instance, a bell, or musical instrument—and that which proceeds from a living creature, animal or human being.

When a bell is struck, we may hear the sound and connect it to a pleasant feeling; but when we hear the cry of an animal, we will, beside our own feelings, detect the manifestation of our own inward experience towards this animal, be that of our pleasure or pain. It is with the latter kind of sounds that we must set to work. **We must concentrate our full attention on the fact that sounds tell us of something that lies outside of our own souls.**

We must immerse ourselves in this foreign entity. We must closely unite our own feelings with the pleasures or pains of which the sound is telling us. We must get beyond the point of caring whether, for us, the sound is pleasant or unpleasant, agreeable or disagreeable; and our soul must be filled with whatever is occurring in our being from which the sounds proceed. Through such an exercise, if systematically and deliberately performed, we will develop within ourselves the faculty of intermingling, as it were, with the being from which the sound proceeds.

If one is sensitive to music one will find it easier, but we should not suppose that a mere sense for music can take the place of inner work. We must learn to feel this way in the face of the whole of nature. This will implant new faculties in the world of our thoughts and feelings. Through her resounding tones, the whole of nature begins to whisper her secrets to us. What were once merely incomprehensible noises to us become by these means the coherent language of nature. And whereas we once only heard sound from the so-called inanimate object, we now become aware of the new languages of our soul.

Should we advance further in this inner culture, we will soon learn that we can hear what once we could not even imagine. We begin to hear with our own souls.

Developing How We Listen to Others

Moving forward, we must now understand the importance of developing how we listen to others. We must accustom ourselves so that, while listening, our inner beings remain silent. When someone else speaks to us, we tend to have a feeling of either our approval or our disapproval. However, our approval or disapproval must be silenced.

We are not expected to suddenly do this at once. In spiritual research, this is always systematically practiced. **Our duty is to listen, by way of practice and at a certain time, to the most contradictory view and—at the same time—bring entirely to silence all assent and, most especially, all adverse criticism.** The point being that by doing so, not only is our intellectual judgment being silenced, but also our feelings of our displeasure, denial, or even assent.

However, we must be very watchful that these feelings—while not on the surface—do not instead still lurk in the innermost part of our soul. By practice, we must listen to the statements of people who are, in some respects, far beneath us, and yet while doing so suppress our feelings of greater knowledge or superiority.

By the way, it is especially useful to listen in this way to children, for even the wisest can learn incalculably much from children.

Of course, this implies the very strictest of self-discipline, but the latter leads us to our higher goals.

When these exercises are practiced in connection with the others already given (dealing with the sounds of nature), our souls develop new senses of hearing. We will now be able to perceive manifestations from the spiritual worlds which do not find their expressions in sounds perceptible to our physical ears. **The perceptions of the "inner words" awaken. Gradually, truths will reveal themselves to us from the spiritual worlds.** We hear speeches uttered to us in spiritual ways. If we hurl any of our personal opinions or feelings against the speaker to whom we are listening, the beings of the spiritual worlds will remain silent to us.

> *"When we practice listening without criticism, even when completely contradictory opinions are spoken, little by little we will learn to blend ourselves with the beings of others by identifying not by our opinions but instead by way of our souls."*

Every sentence of Spiritual Science we hear is there by nature, to direct our mind to a point which must be reached before our soul may experience real progress. In all esoteric trainings, such studies belong to the preparatory periods, and all other methods will prove ineffective if we are not receptive to these teachings. Since these instructions are culled from the living inner words, from living inwardly instilled speeches, they are themselves gifted with spiritual lives. **They are not mere words; they are living powers.** And while we follow the words from those that know, or read books that spring from real inner experiences, powers are working within our own souls, known as clairvoyance.

Stage 2: Enlightenment

"Enlightenment is gained from quite a simple process. Here, too, it is a matter of developing certain feelings and thoughts which slumber in us all and must be awakened."

It is only when this process is carried out with unfailing patience, continuously and conscientiously, that we are led to the perception of our inner light-forms.

The First Steps Towards Enlightenment

The first steps are taken by our observing different natural objects in particular ways; for instance, a transparent and beautifully formed stone, plant, or animal. Here we should try, at first, to direct our entire attention to the comparison of the stone with the animal. Our thoughts should now pass through our soul and be accompanied with vivid feelings. No other thoughts, or feelings, must mingle or disturb this intensely attentive observation.

While comparing, we may say to ourselves: "The stone has a form; the animal also has a form. The stone remains motionless. The animal changes as it moves. It is their instincts (desire) which cause the animal to change places. Instinct, too, is served by the association of the animal to their species and how their organs and limbs are fashioned in accordance with their instincts. The forms of the stone are not fashioned in accordance with desire, but in accordance with a desire-less force."

By sinking deeply into such thoughts and, while doing so,

observing the stone and the animal with our deepest attention, there arises in our soul two separate kinds of feelings. From the stone there flows into our soul one kind of feeling, and from the animal another kind. We will probably not achieve success on our first attempt, but little by little, with genuine and patient practice of this exercise these feelings will ensue.

At first these feelings will only be present as long as the observations last. Later they will continue to grow into something which remains living in our soul. We have but only to reflect upon them, and both feelings will always arise, even without the contemplation of external objects. **Out of these feelings and thoughts, and those which were bound up with them, the organ of our clairvoyance is formed.** If a plant should then be included in this observation, it will be noticed that the feelings flowing from it lie between the feelings derived from the stone and from the animal, both by qualities and by degrees. **The organs thus formed are our spiritual eyes. Through enlightenment, the world becomes light.**

The Spiritual Apprehension of Color

Here it must also be noted that the words "dark" and "light," as well as the other expressions, only approximately describe what is meant, because our language was created to suit our physical conditions.

Spiritual Science describes that which, for the clairvoyant, flows from the stone as "blue" or "blue-red"; and that which is felt coming from the animal as "red" or "red-yellow." Color of a spiritual kind is seen in all possible intermediate shades. A plant is green, which little by little turns into light ethereal pink. Stones, plants, and animals have their own shades of color. **To apprehend color spiritually means to have a sensation like the one experienced when our physical eye rests on that color.**

In addition to this, there are also beings of the higher worlds who never incarnate physically but who have their own colors—often wonderful, often horrible. Indeed, the wealth of color in these higher worlds is immeasurably greater than that in our physical world.

Increasing Our Moral Strength, Inner Purity, and Powers of Observation

Once we have received the capability of seeing with spiritual eyes, we will then encounter, sooner or later, beings—some of them higher, some of them lower than human beings—beings that never enter physical realities. If this point has been reached, experienced guidance is advised.

If we have reached the strength and the endurance to travel so far that we have accomplished these elementary conditions of enlightenment, we will assuredly be able to seek and find the right guidance. But in any circumstance, one precaution is necessary: that we should never lose the qualities of being good and noble, and being receptive to all physical realities.

Throughout these trainings we must continually increase our moral strength, our inner purity, and our powers of observation. For example: during the elementary exercises on enlightenment, we must always take care to enlarge our sympathy for the animal and the human worlds, and raise our senses towards the beauty and wonders of nature. Failing this kind of care, such exercises would continually blunt our feelings, and our hearts would become hardened, and our senses blunted, which could only lead toward perilous results.

During these times, the paths to Spiritual Sciences are sought by many, in many ways; and many dangerous and even despicable practices are attempted. It is necessary that the truth becomes known to prevent errors causing great harm. No harm will ever come to anyone following the way that has been described here—that is, if matters are not forced.

Only one thing needs to be noted: We should never spend more time and strength upon an exercise described than we can spare in regard to the positions in our lives and our personal duties; nor should we start making changes (for the time being) in the external conditions of our lives. Without patience, no genuine results may be attained.

After doing an exercise for a few minutes, we must be able to stop and continue quietly doing our daily work, and no thought of this exercise should intermingle with our work.

"We will never attain results of real value if we have not learned to wait, in the highest and best sense of the word."

Control of Our Thoughts and Feelings

While seeking the path leading to higher knowledge, we must never stop repeating to ourselves that we "should have made considerably more progress after a certain amount of time." The powers and abilities to be developed are of the most subtle and calculated kind. We have been accustomed to occupying ourselves exclusively within the physical world, and the world of our spirits and souls have been concealed from our vision and concepts. It is therefore not surprising if we do not immediately notice the powers of our souls and spirits developing within us.

In this respect, there is the possibility of discouragement for those setting out on the path to higher knowledge. Our guides are aware of our progress long before we are consciously aware. They know how our delicate spiritual eyes begin to form long before we are aware of this, and a great part of what they have to say is coached in such terms, as to prevent us from losing our patience and perseverance before we may gain knowledge of our own progress.

Our guides, as we know, can confer upon us no powers which are not already latent within us; and their sole function is to assist us in the awakening of our slumbering capacities. Our guides, through their own experiences, are pillars of strength for those wishing to penetrate through the darkness to light.

Many have abandoned their paths to higher knowledge soon after having set foot upon them, because their progress was not immediately apparent. And even when these first experiences begin to dawn upon us, we may be apt to regard them only as illusions, because we had formed quite different conceptions of what our experiences were supposed to be.

"Courage and self-confidence are two beacons which must never be extinguished on the path towards higher knowledge. No one will ever travel far who cannot bring themselves to repeat exercises which they have failed, apparently, a countless number of times."

"Long before any distinct perception of progress, there arises from the hidden depths of our soul, feelings that we are on the right path. These feelings should be cherished and fostered, for they can develop into trustworthy guides."

Above all, it is imperative we cancel the idea that any fantastic, mysterious practices are required for the attainment of higher knowledge. It must be clearly realized that starts must be made with our thoughts and feelings, and that these feelings and thoughts must merely be given new direction.

We must say: "In the world of our thoughts and feelings the deepest mysteries lie hidden, only as of yet we have been unable to perceive them."

In the end, it all resolves into the fact that we all carry bodies, souls, and spirits amongst us, and yet we are conscious in a true sense only of our bodies, and not of our souls and spirits. As we progress, we become conscious of our souls and spirits, just as ordinary people are conscious of their own bodies.

Therefore, it is of great importance to give proper direction to our thoughts and feelings in order to develop the perceptions that remain invisible in our ordinary lives.

One of the ways by which this development may be carried out will now be indicated, below. Again, like almost everything else so far explained, it is quite a simple matter. Yet the result will be one of greatest achievement if the necessary devotion and sympathy required is applied.

How to Apply the Necessary Devotion and Sympathy to Enlightenment

We shall now literally place before ourselves small seeds of a plant. While contemplating these objects, we must form with intensity the right kind of thoughts, and through these thoughts develop certain feelings.

In the first place, let us clearly grasp what we are really seeing before our eyes. Let us describe to ourselves the shapes and colors as well as all the other qualities of these seeds. Then let our minds dwell upon the following thoughts: "Out of these seeds, if planted in the soil, plants of complex structures will grow."

Let us build up these plants in our imaginations, and reflect to ourselves together as follows: *"What we are now picturing in our imaginations will later on be enticed from these seeds by the forces of earth and light. If we had before us artificial objects, which imitated the seeds to such deceptive degrees that our eyes could not distinguish them from the real seeds, no forces of earth or light would/could avail to produce from them plants."*

If we thoroughly grasp these thoughts so that they become inward experiences, we will also be able to form the following thoughts and couple them with the right feelings: *"All that will ultimately grow out of the seeds are now secretly enfolded within them as the forces of the whole plants. In the artificial imitations of the seeds there are no such forces present. And yet both appear alike to our eyes."* The real seeds, therefore, contain something invisible which is not present in the imitations.

Let us now fully realize that these invisible somethings will transform themselves later into visible plants of shapes and colors. Let us now ponder this thought: *"The invisible will become visible. If we could not think, then that which will only become visible to us later could not already make its presence felt by us."* Particular stress must be laid on the following point: *"What we think, we must also feel with intensity."*

The thoughts mentioned above must become conscious inner experiences, to the exclusion of all our other thoughts and disturbances. And enough time must be taken to allow these thoughts and feelings to penetrate themselves into our souls. If these exercises are accomplished in the right way, then after time—possibly not until after numerous attempts—inner forces will make themselves present. These forces will create in us new powers of perception.

The Creation of New Powers of Perception

Please note: The trains of thought here indicated have been tested and practiced in esoteric trainings since the earliest of times. Anyone attempting to use other exercises devised by themselves, or of which they may have heard or read at one place or another, will inevitably fall astray and find themselves on the paths of boundless mirages.

Exercise 1: The grains of the seeds will appear as if surrounded by small luminous clouds. In a sensible-supersensible way, they will be felt as kinds of flames. The center of these flames evoke the same feelings we have when under the impression of the color lilac, and the edges of the flame evoke the impression of a bluish tone. **What was formerly invisible to us now becomes visible, for it is created by the powers of the thoughts and feelings that we have stirred to life within ourselves. The plants will not become visible until later, so that the physically invisible now reveals itself in spiritually visible ways.**

It is not surprising that what has been spoken may appear to many as just illusions. They may then ask, "What is the use of such visions and such hallucinations?" And many may fall away and abandon the path. But this is precisely the important point: not to confuse spiritual reality with our imagination at this difficult stage in our progressions. Furthermore, there must be the courage to press onward and not become fearful and faint-hearted.

On the other hand, however, the necessity of maintaining unimpaired and perpetually cultivating the healthy, sound senses which distinguish truths from illusions must be emphasized. One must be fully conscious, and self-control must never be lost while doing these exercises. These exercises must be accompanied by the same sane, sound thinking which is applied to the everyday details of our lives.

Intellectual clarity and earnestness of thought must never for a moment be dulled. The greatest mistake would be made if our mental balance were to become disturbed through doing such exercises, or if we were to become hampered from judging the matters of our daily lives as sanely and as soundly as before.

We should examine ourselves over again and again to find out whether we have remained unaltered and/or become unbalanced in any way. Above all, strict care must be taken not to drift off into random or vague meditations, or to experiment with all kinds of exercises.

The trains of thought here indicated have been tested and practiced in esoteric trainings since the earliest of times. Anyone attempting to use other exercises devised by themselves, or of which they may have heard or read in one place or another, will inevitably fall astray and find themselves on the path of boundless mirages.

Exercise 2: The next exercise is as follows: We shall now place before us plants which have attained the stage of full development. Now let us fill our minds with the thought

that the time will come when these plants will wither and die. *"Nothing will be left of what we now see before us. But these plants will have developed seeds, which, in their turn, will develop into new plants. We again become aware that in what we are seeing are somethings lying hidden in that which we cannot see."*

We now fill our minds entirely with the thought that these plants, with their forms and colors, will in time be no more. But our reflections that they produce seeds teaches us that they will not disappear into nothing.

We cannot presently see with our eyes that which guards them from disappearance, any more than we previously could discern in the plants the grains of their seeds. Thus, there is something in the plants which our eyes cannot see. If we let these thoughts live within us, and if our corresponding feelings are coupled with them, then in due time we will develop in our soul forces that which will ripen into new perceptions.

Out of plants, there again grow a kind of spiritual flame-form, which are, of course, correspondingly larger than the ones which were previously described. These flames can be felt as being greenish-blue in their centers, and yellowish-red at the outer edges.

It must be clearly emphasized that the colors described above are not seen in the same way as our physical eyes see colors. To apprehend blue spiritually means to have sensations like the ones experienced when our physical eyes rest on the color blue. This fact must be noted in order to raise our spiritual perceptions. Otherwise, we expect mere repetitions of the physical in the spiritual. This could only lead to deception.

Having reached this point of spiritual vision, we are richer by a great deal, for we can perceive things not only in their present state, but also in their processes of growth and decay. We begin to see in all things the spirit, of which our physical eyes can know nothing. And therewith we have taken our first steps toward the gradual solution, through our personal vision, of the secrets of our births and our deaths.

"From the outer sense-world, it appears that beings come into existence through their births and pass away through their deaths. This is, however, only because the outer senses cannot perceive the concealed spirits of the beings. For the spirits, births and deaths are merely transformations, just as the unfoldings of the flowers from the buds are transformations enacted before our physical eyes."

But if we have a personal desire to learn this through personal visions, we must first awaken the requisite spiritual senses, as noted.

In order to meet the oppositions which may be raised by certain people who have some psychic experiences, let it at once be noted that there are shorter and simpler ways, and that there are people who have acquired knowledge of the phenomena of birth and death through personal visions, without first going through all that has been described here. There are, in fact, some people with considerable psychic gifts that need only but slight impulses to find themselves already developed. But they are the exceptions, and the methods described above are safer and apply equally to all. It is possible to acquire some knowledge of chemistry in exceptional ways, but if you wish to become a chemist you must follow the recognized and reliable courses.

An error fraught with serious consequences would ensue if it were just assumed that the desired results could be reached more easily if the grains of seeds or the plants mentioned above were merely imagined. These visions thus attained would, in most cases, be mere fragments of the imagination. The exercise is not intended to haphazardly create visions, but to allow reality to create these visions within ourselves. The truth must well up from the depths of our own souls, and must not be conjured forth by our ordinary egos but by the beings themselves whose spiritual truths we are contemplating.

Contemplations of Man Himself
The Three Golden Rules

Once we have found the beginning of our spiritual visions by means of such exercises, we must proceed to the contemplation of man himself. The simple phenomenon of human life must be chosen first. But before making any attempt in this direction, it is imperative to strive for the absolute purity of our own moral characters. We must banish all thoughts of ever using knowledge gained in these ways for our own personal benefits.

We must be convinced that we would never, under any circumstances, avail ourselves in any evil senses of power in order to gain over our fellow-beings. For these reasons, all who seek to discover through their personal visions these secrets must follow the golden rules of true Spiritual Science.

*"For every step that is taken
in the pursuit of higher knowledge,
take three steps toward
the perfection of our own characters."*

If this rule is observed, then this next exercise may follow: Recall to mind some person we may have observed when they were filled with desire for some object. Now direct attention to this desire. It is best to recall to memory the moment when this desire was at its height, and it was still uncertain whether the object of this desire would be attained. And now, we must fill our minds with this recollection and reflect on what we can now observe.

Inner tranquility must be obtained. Every effort must be made to be blind and deaf to everything that may be going on around, and take special heed that through this conception is evoked a feeling of awakening in our souls. Allow these feelings to rise in our soul like clouds on the cloudless horizon.

As a general rule our reflections will be interrupted,

because the person whom we were observing was not observed in this particular state of their soul for a sufficient length of time. Attempts will most likely fail hundreds and hundreds of times. It is just a question of our not losing patience. After many attempts, we will succeed in experiencing feelings in our soul corresponding to the state of the soul of the person being observed.

We will notice that through these feelings, powers grow in our souls that lead us to spiritual insights and into the state of the souls of others. A picture experienced as luminous appears in our field of vision. These spiritually luminous pictures are the so-called astral embodiments of the desire observed in the other's soul.

Much depends on treating such spiritual experiences with great delicacy. To attempt to describe such an experience in inappropriate words may only lead to gross self-deception. The consequence is that in our attempt to clothe these experiences in words, we are misled into blending the actual experience with all kinds of fantastic delusions.

Here again is another important rule to follow:

*"Know how to observe silence
concerning a spiritual experience.
Yes, we must observe silence
even towards ourselves."*

Do not attempt to clothe in words what is contemplated in the spirit with inept intellect. We must lend ourselves freely and without reservation to these spiritual impressions, and not disturb them by reflecting and pondering over them.

Remember that our reasoning capabilities are by no means equal to our new experiences. We have acquired reasoning powers in our lives which were previously confined to the physical world of our senses. Do not try, therefore, to apply these new and higher perceptions to the standards of the old. Only those who have gained some certainty and steadiness in their observations and that of their inner experiences may speak about them, and thereby stimulate their fellow-beings.

The exercise just described may also be supplemented in the following way: Direct your attention in the same way upon a person to whom the fulfillment of some wish, the gratification of some desire, has been granted. If the same rules and precautions are adopted as in the previous instance, spiritual insight will once more be attained.

By such observations of our fellow-beings, we may easily lapse into our moral faults. We may become cold-hearted. All conceivable effort must be made to prevent this. Such observations should only be practiced when we have already risen to the level with complete certainty that these thoughts and rules are real.

We must no longer allow ourselves to think of our fellow-beings in ways that are incompatible with the highest reverence for human dignity and human liberty. The thought that a human being could be a mere object of our observation must never for a moment be entertained. Self-education must see to it that this insight into human nature should go hand-in-hand with the unlimited respect for the personal privilege of all individuals, and with the recognition of the sacred and inviolable nature of that which dwells in all human beings. Feelings of reverential awe must fill our beings, even in our recollections.

How Enlightened Insight May be Achieved

Presently, only these two examples can be given to show how enlightened insight into human nature may be achieved; they will at least serve to point out the ways to be taken.

By gaining the inner tranquility and relaxation indispensable for such observations, we will have undergone great inner transformation. We will then soon reach the point where the enrichments of our inner selves will lend confidence and composure to our outward demeanors. And

these transformations of our outward demeanors will also react favorably on our souls.

Thus, we are able to help ourselves further along our roads. Ways and means of penetrating more and more into the secrets of human nature which are hidden from our external senses will be found, and we will then also have developed the desire for deeper insights into the mysterious connections between human nature and all else that exists in the universe.

What Would-Be Initiates Need to Bring Along

By following these paths, the approach gets closer and closer to the moment in which we may effectively take our first steps of initiation. But before these can be taken, one thing more is necessary, though at first these needs may not be apparent; later on, however, we will become convinced of them.

"Would-be initiates must bring along with them certain measures of courage and fearlessness. They must positively go out of their way to find opportunities for developing these virtues."

Our trainings should provide for systematic cultivation. In this respect, our lives themselves are good schools—possibly the best schools. We must learn to look danger calmly in the face and try to overcome difficulties with determination. For instance, when in the presence of some peril, we must swiftly come to the conviction that fears are of no possible use; we must not feel afraid, and must only think of what is to be done.

And we must improve to the extent of our feelings, upon such occasions which formerly filled us with fear, that to be frightened, to be disheartened, are things that are out of the question as far as our own innermost selves are concerned. By containing our self-discipline in this direction, definite qualities will be developed which are necessary for initiation into the higher mysteries. **Just as nervous forces in our physical beings are required in order to use our physical senses, so we also require in our soul natures those forces which are only developed when we are courageous as well as fearless.**

For in penetrating to the higher mysteries, we will see things which are concealed from ordinary humanity by the illusions of our senses. Our physical senses do not allow us to perceive these higher truths; they are simply our benefactors. Things are thereby hidden from us which, if realized without due preparation, would throw us into complete distress, and the sight of which would be unendurable. We must therefore be fit to endure these sights. We lose certain support in the outer worlds that we owe to the very illusions surrounding us.

The Forces at Work and the Cultivation of Courage and Fearlessness

*"The forces at work in the world
are both destructive and constructive;
the destinies of manifested beings
are our births and deaths.
We are to behold the workings of these forces
and the march of destiny."*

The veils enshrouding our spiritual eyes from which were once our ordinary lives are removed. But men are interwoven with these forces and with their own destinies. Our own natures harbor destructive and constructive forces. Our own souls reveal themselves to us as undisguised as the other objects.

We must not lose strength in the face of self-knowledge, but strength will fail us unless we bring a surplus from which to draw. For this purpose,

"We must learn to maintain our inner calm and steadiness in the face of difficult circumstances; we must cultivate strong trust in the tender powers of existence."

We must be prepared to find that many motives which once drove us before will no longer do so.
We will have to recognize that previously we thought and acted in certain ways only because we were still in the throes of our own ignorance. Reasons that once used to influence us will now disappear. We often acted out of vanity; we will now see how utterly futile all vanity is. We often acted out of greed; we will now become aware of how destructive all greed is. We will have to develop quite new motives for our thoughts and actions, and it is just for these purposes that both courage and fearlessness are required.

It is pre-eminently the question of cultivating courage and fearlessness in the innermost depths of our thought-lives. We must learn to never despair over our failures, and to be equal to the thought: "We shall forget that we have failed in this matter, and shall try once more as though it had never happened." Thus, there will be a struggle through to the firm conviction that the fountainhead of strength from which we may draw is inexhaustible. The struggle will be ever onward to the spirits which will uplift us and support us, however weak and impotent our earthly selves may have proved. We must be capable of pressing on toward the future, undismayed by any experiences of the past.

If these powers have been acquired up to a certain point, we are now ripe to hear the real names of things, which are the key to higher knowledge. Initiation consists in these very acts of learning to call the things of the world by those names which they bear in the spirits of their divine authors. In these, their names, lie the mystery of things. It is for this reason that we as initiates must speak different languages from those who are uninitiated.

Stage 3: Initiation

Initiation is the highest stage in esoteric training, of which is possible to give only some indication in a book intended for the general public. Whatever lies beyond these teachings forms subjects too difficult to understand; but as far as the lesser mysteries are concerned, the ways to this higher knowledge may be found by all who have passed through the stages of *Preparation, Enlightenment, and Initiation.*

The knowledge and proficiency conferred by initiation cannot be obtained in any other manner, except in some far-distant future, after many incarnations, by quite different means and in quite different forms. The secrets of existence are only accessible and correspondent to our own degrees of maturity. For these reasons alone, the path to these higher stages of knowledge and power are beset with obstacles.

Those of us who are initiated today will still lack the experience yet to be gained during our future incarnations. At the portal of initiation, therefore, these experiences must be supplied in some other way. Thus, the first instruction given to candidates for initiation serves as a substitute for these future experiences. These are the so-called trials which we must undergo, and which constitute a normal course of our inner development, resulting from due application to such exercises as described in the preceding chapters.

These trials are often discussed in books, but it is only natural that such discussions should, as a rule, give quite false impressions; for without passing through the stages of preparation and enlightenment, no one can know anything of these tests and appropriately describe them. Would-be initiates must come into contact with certain things and facts belonging to the higher worlds; and they can only see and hear them if their feelings are ripe for perception of the spiritual forms, colors, and tones described in the sections on *Preparation and Enlightenment*.

REVIEW OF THE TRIALS TOWARD ENLIGHTENMENT

The first of these trials consists in our obtaining truer visions than average beings have of the material attributes of lifeless things, and later of plants, animals, and human beings. This does not mean what is presently referred to as "scientific knowledge," for these are not questions of science but rather of visions.

As a rule, a would-be initiate proceeds to learn how the objects of nature and these beings gifted with life manifest themselves to our spiritual ears and our spiritual eyes. In a certain way, these things lie stripped naked before the beholder. These qualities, which can be seen and heard, are hidden from our physical eyes and ears. These physical perceptions are concealed as if by veils, and the falling away of these veils for the would-be initiate is a process designated as the process of *Purification by Fire*. The first trial is therefore known as the *Fire-Trial*.

For many people, their ordinary life is an unconscious process of initiation through the *Fire-Trial*. Such people have passed through a wealth of experience, so that their self-confidence, courage, and fortitude have been greatly strengthened in a normal manner while learning to bear sorrow, disappointment, and failure in their undertakings with greatness of soul, and especially with equanimity and unbroken strength.

Thus, they are often an initiate without knowing it. They then need to acquire extraordinarily little in order to unseal their spiritual hearing and sight so that they become clairvoyant. For it must be noted that a genuine fire-trial is not intended to satisfy the curiosity of a candidate. It is true that they learn many uncommon things of which others can have no inkling;

but the acquisition of this knowledge is not the end, but the *means* to the end. The end consists in the attainment, thanks to this knowledge, of the higher worlds, of greater and truer self-confidence, higher degrees of courage, and magnanimity and perseverance which cannot, as a rule, be acquired in the lower world.

A candidate always has the choice to turn back after the fire-trial. They will then resume their life, strengthened in both body and soul, and wait for a future incarnation to continue their initiation. In their present incarnation, they will prove themselves more useful members of society and of humanity than they were before. In whatever position they may find themselves, their firmness, prudence, resoluteness, and beneficent influence over their fellows will have greatly increased.

But if, after completing the fire-trial, they wish to continue the path, certain writing-systems generally adopted in esoteric training must now be revealed. The actual teachings manifest themselves in these writings, because the hidden (occult) qualities of things cannot be directly expressed in the words of ordinary writing. These occult scripts reveal themselves to our souls when we have attained spiritual perceptions, for they are traced in the spiritual worlds and remain there for all time.

They cannot be learned as artificial writings, nor learned and read. As a candidate, we grow into clairvoyant knowledge in appropriate ways; and during this growth, new strengths are developed in our souls as new functions, through which we feel impelled to decipher the occurrences and beings of these spiritual world-like characters of writings.

These strengths, with the experiences that they bring, might possibly awaken in our souls as though they were of our own accord, as our souls are continually developing. But it is safer to follow these instructions from those who are spiritually experienced, and who have some proficiency in deciphering these occult scripts.

> *"The signs of the occult scripts were not arbitrarily invented; they correspond to the forces actively engaged in the world. They teach us the language of things. It becomes immediately apparent to us that the signs that we are now learning correspond to the forms, colors, and tones which we learned to perceive during the stages of Preparation and Enlightenment. We realize that all we have previously learned was only like our learning to spell, and that we are only now beginning to read the higher worlds."*

All the isolated figures, tones, and colors reveal themselves to us now in one great connected whole. Now, for the first time, we attain complete certainty in our observation of the higher worlds. Before this, we would not have known positively whether these things we see are rightly seen. Thanks to this language, we also learn certain rules of conduct and certain duties of which we formerly knew nothing.

Having previously learned these rules and duties, the actions we perform now are endowed with significance and meaning that those who are not initiated could never possess. We act out of the higher worlds. Instructions concerning such actions can only be read and understood in the occult scripts.

Yet it must be emphasized that there are people who are unconsciously gifted with the abilities and faculties of performing such actions, though they have never undergone any esoteric training.

Such helpers of the world and of humanity pass through life bestowing blessings and performing good deeds. For reasons not to be discussed here, gifts have been bestowed on them which appear supernatural. What distinguishes them from us is only that they are acting consciously and with full insight and can see the full picture. They acquire by training these gifts bestowed on others by higher powers for the good of humanity. We can sincerely revere these favored of God; but we should not for these reasons regard the work of esoteric trainings as something extra.

Once we have learned the sign-language, there awaits us yet another trial, and that is to prove whether we can move with freedom and assurance in the higher worlds.
In our ordinary lives, we are impelled to action by exterior motives. We work at one occupation or another because one duty or another is imposed on us by our outward circumstances.

It need not be mentioned that we must never neglect any of our duties in our ordinary lives because we are living and working in higher worlds. There is no duty in the higher world that can force us to neglect any single one of our duties in the ordinary world. On the contrary, all those qualities which make human beings more capable and efficient, are more enhanced by those who have been initiated and are incomprehensible to those who have not.

At this stage of our initiation, we must not be moved to any action by external pressures, but only adhere to the rules of conduct revealed in the occult scripts. We must now show in this second trial that, led by such rules, we can act with the same firmness and precision with which, for instance, officials perform their duties. For this purpose, and during our further trainings, we will find ourselves faced by certain definitive tasks.

We must perform actions in sequence with the observations made based on what has been learned during the stages of Preparation and Enlightenment. Our actions are understood by means of the occult scripts with which we have now been familiarized.

If our duties are recognized and we act rightly, our trials have been successful. Our progression is recognized in the revisions produced by our actions in figures, colors, and tones apprehended by our spiritual eyes and ears. Exact indications will be offered as our training progresses, showing how these figures appear and how they are experienced after actions have been performed.

The Water-Trial

How to produce these changes: **This trial is known as the *Water-Trial*, because in this activity in the higher worlds, would-be candidates are deprived of the support derived from outward circumstances,** as swimmers are without support when swimming in water that is beyond their depths. These activities must be repeated until absolute poise and assurance have been attained.

The importance of this trial lies in the acquisition of certain qualities. Through experiences in the higher worlds, these qualities will be developed in such a short time and to such a high degree, that one would otherwise have to go through many incarnations before they could acquire them to the same extent.

The central factor is that we must be guided to produce these higher regions of existence only by the results of higher perception, and the readings of the occult scripts. Should, in the course of our activities, we introduce any of our own opinions and desires, or should we diverge for one moment from the laws which we have recognized to be right in order to follow our own willful inclinations, then the results produced will differ entirely from what was intended. We would lose sight of the goals to which our actions are tended, and confusion would result.

Hence, ample opportunity is given during this trial to develop self-control. **Here again, this trial can be more easily passed by those whose lives, before initiation, had led them to acquire self-control.** Anyone having acquired the ability of following higher principles and ideals, while putting into the background all personal devises; anyone capable of always performing their duties even though their feelings would like to seduce them from these duties—such people are unconsciously initiates in the midst of their ordinary lives. They will need but little to succeed in these trials.

Indeed, certain measures of initiation are unconsciously

acquired in our lives and, as a rule, will be indispensable for success in this second trial. For even as it may appear difficult for those who have not learned to spell in their childhoods to make good of these deficiencies when they are fully grown, so too it is difficult to develop the necessary degrees of self-control at the moment of looking into the higher worlds, if these abilities have not been acquired to certain a degree in our ordinary lives. The objects of the physical world do not alter the nature of our wishes, desires, and inclinations. In the higher worlds, however, our wishes, desires, and inclinations are causes that produce effects. If we wish to produce effects in these worlds, we must strictly follow the right rules and subdue all our willful impulses.

The Importance of the Use of Sound Judgment

One of the human qualities that is of special importance at this stage of initiation is *unquestionably sound judgment.* **Attention should have been placed on the training of these senses during all the previous stages, for it now remains to be proven whether candidates are shaping ways that show them to be fit for the true paths of knowledge. Further progress is now only possible if all illusions, superstitions, and everything fantastic can be distinguished from true realities.**

This is, at first, more difficult to accomplish in the higher stages of existence than in the lower stages. Every prejudice, every cherished opinion regarding the things in question, must vanish; truth alone must be the guide. There must be perfect readiness to abandon immediately any ideas, opinions, or inclinations when our logical thoughts demand them. Our personal opinions are never to be considered.

The knowledge of the higher worlds opens precious treasures that are all able to acquire. With the removal of all doubt regarding these higher worlds, all will be revealed. But these treasures cannot be acquired so long as we are the prey of illusions. It would indeed be fatal if our imaginations and prejudices were to run away with our intellects. Dreamers and fantastical people are as unfit for these paths to higher knowledge as are superstitious people.

This cannot be over-emphasized, for the most dangerous of enemies on the way to this knowledge of the higher worlds lurks in such foolish studies and superstitions. Yet we need not have to believe that we lose all sense of poetry in our lives, all powers of enthusiasm just because the words *"We must be rid of all prejudices"* are written over the portal leading to the second trial of initiation, and because over the portal at the entrance to the first trial we read: *"Without normal common sense, all thine efforts are in vain."*

A third trial awaits, if we are sufficiently advanced in these ways. And that is: There are no definite goals to be reached. All that is left is in our own hands. We must find our way all alone and out of ourselves.

Things or people are not there to stimulate us into action. Nothing and nobody can give us the strength we need, as we ourselves are alone. Failure to find the inner strength will leave us standing where we are. Few of those who have successfully passed the previous trials will fail to find the necessary strength at this point. All that is acquired by now is the ability to come quickly to terms with ourselves, for we must here find our *higher selves* in the truest sense of the words.

We must rapidly decide in all things to listen to the inspirations of the spirits. There is no time for doubt or hesitation. Every moment of hesitation would prove us to still be unfit. Whatever prevents us from listening to the voices of the spirits must be courageously overcome.

It is a question of showing presence of mind in these situations. The training at this stage is concerned with the perfect development of this quality. All accustomed inducements to act or even to think now cease. In order not to remain inactive, we must not lose ourselves; for only within ourselves can we find the central points of vantage where we can gain a firm hold. Upon reading this, no one without further acquaintance with these matters should feel any opposition toward these principles being thrown back at them, for success in these trials brings with them moments of supreme happiness.

Our Ordinary Lives Are our Esoteric Trainings

At this stage no less than any of the others, our ordinary lives are our esoteric trainings. Having reached this point, we should be able, when suddenly confronted with some task or problem, to come to a swift decision without any hesitation or delay. Such situations are instantly lost if actions are not rapid. When we are able to take quick action when misfortune is imminent, whereas a few moments of hesitation would have seen this misfortune as an accomplished fact, we have turned our ability into a permanent personal quality and we have unconsciously acquired the degree of maturity necessary for the third trial.

The Air-Trial
Absolute Presence of Mind

At this stage, everything centers around the development of keeping absolute presence of mind. This trial is known as the *Air-Trial*. While undergoing it, we support ourselves neither from the external incentives nor from the figures, tones, and colors which we had learned at the stages of *Preparation* and *Enlightenment*, but depend exclusively upon ourselves. Upon successfully passing this trial, we are permitted to enter the *Temple of Higher Wisdom*.

The task now to be performed is to take an oath never to betray anything that has been learned. The expressions, "oath" and "betray," may be misleading. There is no actual taking of an oath in the ordinary sense of the word, but rather the experience that comes at this stage of development. It is here where a candidate must learn how to apply the higher knowledge, and how to place it at the service of humanity.

It is here that we begin to really and truly understand the world. It is not so much the question of withholding the higher truths, but far more of our serving them in the right way and with the necessary tact. The silence we are to keep refers to something quite different. We acquired these finer qualities with regard to things which had previously been spoken, and especially with regard to the manner in which they were spoken. We would be poor initiates if we did not place all the higher knowledge we have acquired at the service of humanity, as well and as far as this is possible.

The only obstacle in giving information in this matter is the lack of understanding on the part of the recipient. It is true, of course, that this higher knowledge does not lend itself to unrestrained talking; but no one who has reached this stage of development is actually forbidden to say anything.

No other person, no other being, may obtain from us any oath with this intent. Everything is left to our own responsibility, and we learn in all situations to discover within ourselves what we have to do. So the oath means nothing more than that we have been found qualified to be entrusted with such responsibility.

Draught of Forgetfulness into the Secret Knowledge

If we are fit candidates for the foregoing experience, we are then given what is called symbolically the "draught of forgetfulness." This means that when we are initiated into the secret knowledge, we are enabled to act without being continually disturbed by our lower memories. It is necessary for an initiate to have full faith in the immediate present. We must be able to destroy the veil of memories which envelop us at all moments of our lives. If we judge something that happens to us today according to the experiences of yesterday, we are exposed to multitude of errors.

Of course, this does not mean that the experiences gained

in our lives should be renounced. They should always be kept in our minds as clearly as possible. But as an initiate, we must have the ability to judge all new experiences wholly according to what is inherent in them, and let them react upon us unobscured by their pasts.

"We must be prepared at all moments that all objects and all beings may bring to us some new revelation. If we judge the new by the standards of the old, we are liable to error. Our past experiences are of greatest use for the very reason that they enable us to perceive the new. If we had not gone through definite experiences, we would perhaps be blind to the qualities of the objects or beings that come before us."

Thus, our experiences should serve the purpose of perceiving the new and not judging them by the standards of the old. In this respect, as initiates we acquire certain definite qualities, and thereby many things are revealed to us which remain concealed from the uninitiated.

Draught of Remembrance into the Secret Knowledge

The second draught presented to initiates is the draught of remembrance. Through this action, we acquire the faculty of retaining the knowledge of the higher truths that are ever-present in our souls.

Our ordinary memories would be unequal to this task.

*"We must unite ourselves and become as one
with the higher truths.
We must not only know them,
but also be able as a matter of course
to manifest and administer them
into living action."*

They must become our practices, our habits, our inclinations.

There must be no need to keep thinking about them in our ordinary senses. They must come as living expressions unto themselves; they must flow through us as functions of ourlives through our organisms. *Thus we ever raise ourselves, in the spiritual sense, to the same status to which nature raises itself in the physical sense.*

– Chapter 3 –

SOME PRACTICAL ASPECTS

The training of our thoughts and feelings, pursued in the ways described in Chapter 2 on *Preparation, Enlightenment, and Initiation,* **introduce into our souls and spirits the same organic symmetries with which nature constructed our physical bodies.** Before these developments, our souls and spirits were indistinguishable masses.

Clairvoyants perceive this as interlacing, rotating, cloud-like spirals, dully glimmering in reddish, reddish-browns, or reddish-yellow tones. After these trainings, the symmetries and the masses begin to assume brilliant yellowish-green or greenish-blue colors and show regular structures. These inner regularities leading to higher knowledge are attained when they are introduced into our thoughts and feelings in the same orderly systems with which nature has endowed our bodily organs that enable us to see, hear, digest, breathe, and speak. Gradually, we learn to breathe and see with our souls, and to speak and hear with the spirits.

In the following pages, some practical aspects of the higher education of our souls and spirits will be treated in greater detail. They are such that anyone can put them into practice regardless of other rules, and thereby be led some distance further into Spiritual Science.

The Important Quality of Patience

Particular effort must be made to cultivate the quality of patience. All symptoms of impatience produce paralyzing, even destructive, effects on the higher capacities that slumber within us. We must not expect immeasurable views into the higher worlds from one day to the next, or we most assuredly will be disappointed. We must be contented with even the smallest fragments attained, and allow repose and tranquility to take more possession of our souls.

It is quite understandable to await results with impatience; but nothing will be achieved so long as we fail to master all impatience. Nor is it of any use to seek to combat any impatience in the ordinary sense of the word, for impatience will become only that much stronger. We overlook it in self-deception while it plants itself firmly in the depths of our souls. It is only when we surrender ourselves to certain definite thoughts, making them absolutely our own, that any results may be attained.

The thought to cultivate is as follows:

*"We must do everything we can for
the training and development
of our souls and spirits;
but we must wait patiently
until higher powers shall have
found us worthy of definite enlightenment.
If this thought becomes so powerful that
it grows into actual features of our character,
then we are treading the right path."*

This feature soon sets its mark on our exterior. The gaze of our eyes becomes steady, the movement of our body becomes sure, our decisions become definite, and all that goes under the name of "nervousness" gradually disappears.

Even rules that appear trifling and insignificant must be considered. For example, suppose that someone affronts us. Before our trainings, we would have most probably directed our resentment against the offender; waves of anger would have surged up within us. In light of the training, however, in similar cases, these thoughts immediately present in our minds that such offensives make no difference to our intrinsic worth. And we do whatever must be done to meet these offenders with our calm and composure, and not in a spirit of anger.

Of course, it is not a case of simply accepting every offender, but of our acting with the same calm composure when dealing with offensives against our own person as we would if the offender were directing them against another person, in whose favor we had the right to intervene. It must always be remembered that these trainings are not carried out in a crude outward process, but in subtle, silent alterations in the lives of our thoughts and feelings.

Patience has the effect of attraction on the treasures of higher knowledge, impatience the effect of repulsion. In the higher regions of existence, nothing can be attained by haste and unrest. Above all things, desires and cravings must be silenced, for these are qualities of the soul before which all higher knowledge shyly withdraws. However precious this knowledge is accounted, we must not crave it if we wish to attain it. If we wish to have it for our own sake, we will never attain it.

This requires us to be honest with ourselves in our innermost souls. We must not, in any cases, be under any illusions concerning our own selves. With these feelings and inner truths in our awareness, we must look at our own faults, weaknesses, and unfitness fully in the face. The moment we try to excuse ourselves out of any of our weaknesses, we place a stone on the path which leads us upward. Such obstacles can only be removed by self-enlightenment.

There is only one way to get rid of our faults and failings, and that is by our clear recognition of them. Everything that slumbers in human souls can be awakened. People can even improve their intellects and reasoning abilities, if they quietly and calmly make it clear to themselves why they are weak in these respects. Such self-knowledge is, of course, difficult, for the temptation towards self-deception is immeasurably great.

Yet anyone who makes a habit of being inwardly truthful opens the portals leading to deeper insight.

All idle curiosity must fall away. We must rid ourselves as much as possible of the habit of asking questions merely for the sake of gratifying our own selfish thirst for knowledge, and instead only ask questions when knowledge can serve to perfect our own being in the service of evolution. Nevertheless, our delight in this knowledge and our devotion to it should in no way be hampered. We should listen devoutly to all that contributes to such ends and should seek all opportunity for such devotional attention.

Special attention must be paid in our esoteric training to the education of the life of our desires. This does not mean that we are to become free of desires, for if we are to attain something we must also desire it; however, desire will always tend to fulfillment if backed by particular forces. These forces are derived from right knowledge. *Therefore, do not desire at all until you know what is right in any one sphere.* **That is one of the golden rules. Wise people first ascertain the laws of the world, and then their desires become powers which realize themselves.**

The following example brings this out clearly:
There are certainly many people who would like to learn from their own observations, something about their lives before their birth. However, such desires are altogether useless and lead to no results, so long as the person in question has not acquired knowledge of the laws that govern the nature of the eternal—knowledge of these laws in their subtlest and most intimate character. But if, having really acquired this knowledge, they wish to proceed further, then their desires—now ennobled and purified—will enable them to do so.

It is also no use in saying: "I must particularly wish to examine my previous lives and shall study only for these purposes." We must rather be capable of abandoning these desires, of eliminating them altogether, and of studying at first with no such intentions. We should cultivate feelings of joy and devotion for what we learn, with no thought of the above ends in view. We should learn to cherish and foster our desires in such a way that brings with them our own fulfillment.

"If we become angered, vexed, or annoyed, we erect walls around ourselves in the soul-worlds, and the forces which are to develop the eyes of our souls cannot approach."

For instance, a person who angers us sends forth psychic currents into the soul-worlds. We cannot see these currents if we ourselves are capable of anger. Our own anger conceals them from us. We must not, however, suppose that when we are free from anger we shall immediately have psychic (astral) visions. Our organs of vision must have been developed in our souls. The beginnings of such organs lie latent in all human beings but remain ineffective if we are capable of anger.

We must rather persevere in combating anger, and proceed patiently on our way; then some day we shall find that the eyes of our souls have become developed. Of course, anger is not the only failing to be combated for the attainment of these ends. Many grow impatient or skeptical because they have, for years, combated certain qualities and yet clairvoyance has not ensued. In these cases, they have just trained some qualities and allowed others to run riot.

The gift of clairvoyance only manifests itself when all those qualities which stunt the growth of our latent faculties are suppressed. Undoubtedly, the beginning of such seeing and hearing may appear at earlier periods, but these are only young and tender shoots which are subject to all possible errors—shoots which, if not carefully tended and guarded, may quickly die.

There are other qualities, such as anger and vexation, that have to be combated: those of timidity, superstition, prejudice, vanity, ambition, curiosity, mania for imparting information, and the making of any distinction in human beings according to their outward characteristics based on their rank, sex, race, and so forth.

In our times, it is difficult for people to understand how the combating of such qualities can have anything to do with the heightening of the senses of our cognitions. But every spiritual scientist knows that more depends upon such matters than upon the increase of our intelligence and our employment of artificial exercises.

Misunderstanding may arise if we feel that we must become foolhardy in order to be fearless; that we must close our eyes to the differences between people, because we must combat these prejudices based on rank, race, and so forth. **The truth is that the correct estimate of all things is attained only when we are no longer entangled in our own prejudices.** Even in an ordinary sense, it is true that the fear of some phenomenon prevents us from estimating it correctly; that racial prejudice prevents us from seeing into another person's soul.

Every word that is spoken without first having been thoroughly purged in our thoughts is a stone thrown in the way of our esoteric training. And here, something must be considered which can only be explained by example. If anything is said to which we must reply, we must be careful to consider the speaker's opinions, feelings, and even their prejudices, rather than what we ourselves have to say at this moment of discussion. This does not mean that we must withhold our opinions. There can be no question of that. But we must listen to the speaker as carefully and as attentively as we possibly can and let our replies derive from what we have just heard. **The importance lies not in the difference of our opinions but in our discovering through our own efforts whether we should contribute something towards it.**

Thoughts of these kinds and of a similar nature, cause our characters and behaviors to be permeated with qualities of gentleness, which are one of the chief means used in all esoteric trainings. Harshness scares away soul-pictures that open the eyes of our souls; gentleness clears the obstacles away and unseals these inner organs.

Along with gentleness, other qualities will be developed

in our souls: those of quietly paying attention to all the subtleties in the soul-lives of our environments, while reducing to absolute silence any activities within our own souls.

The soul-life of our environment will impress itself upon us in such a way that our own soul will grow; and as it grows, it becomes regular in its structure, just like a plant expanding in the sunlight. Gentleness and patient reserve open our soul to the soul-worlds and our spirit to the spirit-worlds.

We must persevere in our silent inner seclusion; close our senses to all that they brought us before our training; reduce to absolute immobility all those thoughts which, according to our previous habits, surged within us; become quite still and silent within. We must wait in patience. And then the higher worlds will begin to fashion and perfect the organs of our sight and hearing in our souls and spirits.

We should not immediately expect to see and hear in the world of our soul and spirit, for all that we are doing does but contribute to the development of our higher senses. We will only be able to hear with our soul and spirit when we possess these higher senses.

Having persevered through these times of silent inner seclusion, we are to go about our customary daily affairs, imprinting deeply upon our minds the thought: *"Someday, when I have grown sufficiently, I shall attain that which I am destined to attain";* and we should make no attempt to forcefully attract any of these higher powers for our own sake. We receive these instructions at the outset. By observing them, we perfect ourselves. If we neglect them, all our labors are in vain. This is only a difficult achievement should we become impatient and un-persevering.

> *"No other obstacles exist,*
> *save those which we ourselves place*
> *in the way of our own paths,*
> *which can be avoided by our own wills."*

This point must be continually emphasized, because many people form an altogether wrong conception of the difficulty that may beset the path to higher knowledge. There are other ways which may lead more quickly to these goals; but what is explained here has nothing to do with them, because they have certain effects which no experienced spiritual scientist would consider desirable.

Since fragmentary information concerning these ways is continually finding its way into public life, express warnings must be given against entering upon them. For reasons which only the initiated can understand, these ways can never be made public in their truest forms. These fragments can never lead to profitable results, but may easily undermine a person's health, happiness, and peace of mind. It would be far better for people to avoid having anything to do with such things than to risk entrusting themselves to wholly dark forces, of whose natures and origins they know nothing.

Anyone practicing in an environment filled only with self-seeking interests must be conscious of the fact that these interests are not without their effects on the development of their spiritual organs. Just as lilies can never grow into thistles, so too, the eyes of our souls can never grow into anything but their destined shapes. Under all circumstances, we should now and again seek in our environments the restful peace, the inner dignity, and the sweetness of nature.

Especially fortunate are those who can carry out their esoteric training surrounded by the green worlds of plants, or among the sunny hills, where nature weaves her webs of sweet simplicity. These environments develop our inner organs in a harmony which can never ensue in a modern city.

More favorably situated than the townsman are the persons who, during their childhood, at least, had been able to breathe the fragrance of pines, to gaze on snowy peaks, and to observe the silent activity of woodland creatures and insects. Yet city-dwellers will not fail if they give to the organs of their souls and spirits, as they develop, the nurturing that comes from the inspired teachings of spiritual research.

If our eyes cannot follow the woods in their mantels of green every spring, day by day, we should instead open our souls to the glorious teachings of the Bhagavad Gita, or of St. John's Gospel, or of St. Thomas à Kempis. There are many ways to the summit of our insights, but much depends on right choices.

The spiritually experienced could say much concerning these paths, much that might seem strange to the uninitiated. For instance, when we are very far advanced on our paths—and possibly standing, so to speak, at the very entrance of seeing and hearing souls and spirits—we are then fortunate enough to make our journey over the calm (or maybe tempestuous) oceans, and veils fall away from our eyes and our souls. Suddenly, we become seers.

Some are so far advanced that their veils need only be loosened; this occurs through some stroke of destiny. For others, these strokes might well have had the effect of paralyzing their power and undermining their energy; but for esoteric students, this becomes the occasion of their *enlightenment*. Others persevere patiently for years without any marked results. Suddenly, while silently seated in their quiet chamber, spiritual lights envelop them; the walls disappear, and new worlds expand before their eyes—that of seeing, or resound in their ears—that of spiritually hearing.

– CHAPTER 4 –

THE CONDITIONS OF ESOTERIC TRAINING

The conditions attached to esoteric training are not arbitrary. They are the natural outcomes of esoteric knowledge. Just as we cannot become a painter if we refuse to handle a paintbrush, so, too, we cannot receive esoteric training if we are unwilling to meet the demands considered necessary by our teachers. Our teachers can give nothing but advice, and everything they say should be accepted in this sense. They have already passed through the preparatory stages leading to the knowledge of the higher worlds, and they know from their own experiences what is necessary.

It depends entirely upon our own independent free will whether we choose to tread the same paths. If we were to insist on being admitted to esoteric training without fulfilling these conditions, it would be equivalent to saying: "Teach me how to paint, but do not ask me to handle a paintbrush." Our teachers can never offer anything unless we, as the recipients, come forward to meet them out of our own free will.

But it must be emphasized that just generally desiring this higher knowledge is not sufficient in and of itself. These desires will, of course, be felt by many; but nothing can be achieved so long as the special conditions attached to these esoteric trainings are not accepted. This point should be considered by those who complain that these trainings are difficult. Failure or unwillingness to fulfill these strict conditions will necessitate in the abandonment of the esoteric trainings, for at least the time being. It is true that the conditions are strict; yet they are not harsh, since the fulfillment not only should be but indeed must be by our own voluntary actions.

If this fact is overlooked, any esoteric training will easily appear as a coercion on our soul and on our conscience; for these trainings are based on the development of our inner lives, and our teachers give advice concerning these inner lives.

There is no question of any kind of coercion when these demands are met out of our own free will. To ask of our teacher, "Give me your higher knowledge, but leave me to my customary emotions, feelings, and thoughts," would be an impossible demand. In this case, the gratification of our own curiosity and desire for knowledge would be our only motive. When pursued in this way, higher knowledge can never be attained. Let us now consider, in turn, the conditions imposed.

It must be emphasized that complete fulfillment of any one of these conditions is not insisted upon, but only the corresponding effort. No one can wholly fulfill them, but everyone can start on the paths towards them. It is the effort of our own free will that matters, and our ready disposition to enter upon these paths.

The Seven Conditions towards Higher Knowledge

1. **The first condition is that** *we should pay heed to the advancement of our bodily and spiritual health.* Of course, our spiritual health does not depend upon us just as an individual, but on our effort to advance within the scope of all. Sound knowledge proceeds from sound human beings. The unhealthy are not rejected, but it is demanded that a student should have the will to lead a healthy life.

Each of us must endeavor to take care of ourselves. From the physical aspect, it will be more of a question of warding off harmful influences than of anything else. Duty, in many cases, may stand higher than our health at times; but our own pleasures must never stand higher. Our pleasures must only be a means to our overall health and to our lives, and in these connections we must, above all, be honest and truthful with ourselves.

Many attribute their circumstances as preventing them from making any progress. However, every kind of work can serve the whole of humanity. Of special importance is the striving for complete health of our minds. Unhealthy tendencies in our thoughts and feelings will obstruct our paths towards higher knowledge. Clear, calm thinking, with stability in feelings and emotions, form the foundation for all our work.

Nothing should be removed more than any inclination toward a fantastical, excitable life, or towards exaggeration and extremism. We should acquire a healthy outlook in all circumstances of our lives; we should meet the demands of our lives with steady assurance, quietly letting all things make their impression on us and revealing their messages.

Any one-sided extravagant tendency in sentiment and criticism should be avoided. Failing this, we would find our way merely into a world of our own imagination instead of into the higher worlds; in place of the truth, our own petty opinions would assert themselves. It is better for us to be matter-of-fact than excitable and fantastic.

2. The second condition is that *we should feel synchronized in the whole of life.* Much is included in the fulfillment of this condition, but each one of us may only fulfill it in our own way. If teachers have pupils who do not fulfill their expectations, they must not divert any of their resentments against them, but rather against themselves.

They must feel themselves as one with the pupils, to the extent of asking themselves: "Are my pupil's deficiencies not the result of my own actions? Instead of directing my feelings against them, I should reflect on my own attitudes so that my pupils may in the future be better able to satisfy these demands." Proceeding from such an attitude, changes will come over our entire way of thinking. This holds true in all things, great or small.

Such an attitude of mind may alter the way we regard, for instance, criminals. In that case, we suspend our judgments and say to ourselves: "We are, like them, only human beings.

Through our own favorable circumstances, we may have received an education which perhaps saved us from a similar fate." We may then also conclude that these human brothers of ours would have become different people, had our teachers taken the same pains with them as they have taken upon us.

We shall reflect on the fact that something was given to us which was withheld from them; that we were offered something that had been denied them. **And then we shall naturally come to think of ourselves as links in the whole of humanity, and as sharers in the responsibility for everything that occurs.** This should be cherished within the inner stillness of our souls. Then quite gradually, this will set their mark on our outward demeanors. Each of us may only begin by reforming them within ourselves.

It is of no benefit, in the sense of the previous thoughts, to make general demands on all humanity. It is easier to decide what men "ought" to be; but we are working among the depths, not on the surface. It would therefore be quite wrong for us to relate these demands with external, least of all political, demands; these trainings have nothing to do with such matters. Political agitators know, as a rule, what to demand of other people; but they place little, if any, demands on themselves.

3. The third condition is that we must work our way upward to the realization that *our thoughts and feelings are as important for the world as are our actions.* It must be realized that it is equally as injurious to hate a fellow-being as to strike them. This realization allows us to believe that by perfecting ourselves, we accomplish something not only for ourselves but also for the entire world. The world derives equal benefit from our untainted feelings and thoughts and from our good demeanors. If we do not believe in cosmic importance in our inner lives, we are unfit for the paths thus described. We must admit that all our feelings produce effects, just as do the actions of our own hands.

4. The fourth condition is that we must acquire the conviction that *our real beings do not live in our exterior but in our*

THE CONDITIONS OF ESOTERIC TRAINING

interior. All who regard themselves as a product of their outer world and as a result of their physical world cannot succeed in this esoteric training. We must learn that one cannot be directly measured by the other.

We must find the proper means between what is indicated by our external conditions and what we recognize as the right conduct inside ourselves. We should not force upon our environments anything for which we have no real understanding; but also, we must be quite free from the desire to do only what can be appreciated by those around us.

We must learn as much as we possibly can from our environments to discover what those around us need, and what is good for them. In this way, we will develop within ourselves what is known as "spiritual balance." An open heart for the needs of the outer world lies on one side of the scale, and an inner fortitude and unfaltering endurance on the other.

5. The fifth condition is that we must be *unwavering in carrying out resolutions*. Nothing should encourage us to deviate from any resolution we may have taken, save only those perceptions that we found were in error. **Every resolution we make is a force, and if these forces do not produce immediate effects at the point to which they were applied, they work nevertheless in their own ways.** Success is only significant when our actions arise from our desires. But all actions arising from desires are worthless in relation to the higher worlds. There, *love for our actions are alone the decisive factors. Every impulse that impels us to action should fulfill us with love.* Undismayed by our failures, we will never grow weary of endeavoring repeatedly to translate solutions into actions. And in this way we reach the stage of not waiting to see the outward effects of our actions, and are contented with performing them. We learn to sacrifice our actions, even our entire beings, to the world. Readiness for sacrifice, for offerings such as these, must be shown by all who pursue these paths of esoteric training.

6. The sixth condition is the development of our feelings of thankfulness for everything with which we are favored. *We* *must realize that our existence is a gift from the entire universe,* that which is needed in order to enable each one of us to receive and maintain our existence. How much do we not owe to nature and to our fellow human beings! Thoughts such as these must come naturally for those who seek esoteric training, for if we do not feel inclined to entertain these thoughts, we are incapable of developing within ourselves the all-embracing love which is necessary for our attainment of the higher knowledge. Nothing may reveal this knowledge to us which we do not love. And every revelation we make must fill us with thankfulness, for it is we ourselves who become the richer for it.

    7. **The seventh condition (for all these conditions must be united in a seventh) is that** *we must regard life unceasingly in the manner demanded by these conditions.* We must make it possible to give our lives the stamp of uniformity. All our modes of expression will, in these ways, be brought into harmony, and no longer contradict each other.

    Anyone who sincerely shows the good will to fulfill these conditions may decide to seek esoteric training and will then be ready to follow the advice given above. **Much of this advice may appear to be merely on the surface, and many will perhaps say that they did not expect the training to proceed by means of such strict methods. But** *"everything interior must manifest itself in exterior ways; and just as pictures are not evident when they exist only in the minds of the painters, so, too, there can be no esoteric trainings without outward expressions."* Disregard for these strict methods are only shown by those who do not know that the exterior is the avenue of expression for the interior. No doubt it is the spirits that really matter and not these methods; but just as these methods without spirits are null and void, so also would spirits remain inactive if we did not go through these manners for ourselves.

    The above conditions are calculated to render us strong enough to fulfill the further demands made upon us during our training. If we fail in these conditions, we will hesitate before each new demand, and without them we will lack that faith in mankind which we must possess. For all our strivings for truth must be founded on our faith in and our true love for mankind.

These are the foundations, not the sources, of our striving for the truth; for such strivings may only flow from our own soul's fountainhead of strength. And our love for mankind must gradually widen to our love for all living creatures, and for all existence. We must train ourselves that not only in our actions but also in our words, feelings, and thoughts, we will never destroy anything for the sake of destruction.

We will then see more and more clearly that evil and imperfection may best be combated by the creation of the good and the perfect.

We know that out of nothing, nothing can be created, but also that the imperfect can be transformed into the perfect. If we can develop within us the disposition to create, we will soon find ourselves capable of facing evil in the correct ways.

We must clearly realize that the purpose of these trainings is for us to build, and not to destroy. We should therefore bring with us the good will for sincere and devoted work, with no intention to criticize and destroy. We should be capable of devotion. We must now learn what we do not yet know, which we look reverently on being disclosed to us in the future. Work and our devotion—these are the fundamental qualities which are demanded of us. Some may come to think that they are not progressing, although in their own opinion they are untiringly active.

"Our joy must be in growth and life, and we must only lend our hands to destruction when we are also able—through and by means of destruction—to promote new life. This does not mean that we must simply look on while evil runs riot, but rather that we must seek even in evil that side through which we may transform it into good."

The reason is that they have not yet grasped the meaning of their work and devotion in the correct way. Work done for the sake of our own success will be the least successful, and any learning pursued without devotion will be the least conducive to our progress. *Only the love of our work, and not of our success, will lead us to progress.* And if in our learning we are using our straight thinking and sound judgment, we need not stunt our devotion by these kinds of doubts and suspicions.

Anyone who has advanced some way in the attainment of higher knowledge knows that they owe everything to their quiet attention and active reflection, and not to willful personal judgment. We should always bear in mind that we do not need to learn what we are already able to judge. Therefore, if our sole intention is to judge, we will learn nothing more. If we are unable to understand something, it is far better for us not to judge than for us to judge adversely.

We must wait until later to acquire the true understanding. The higher we climb the ladder of knowledge, the more we require the capability of listening with quiet devotion. All perceptions of the truth, all lives and activities in the world of the spirits, become subtle and delicate in comparison with the process of our ordinary intellect and life in the physical world.

The more the scope of our activity widens out before us, the more delicate the process in which we are engaged. It is for this reason that people arrive at such different opinions and points of view regarding the higher regions. But there is one, and only one, opinion regarding the higher truths; and this one opinion is within reach of all who, through work and devotion, have so risen that they can really behold these truths and contemplate them.

Opinions differing from the one true opinion can only be arrived at when we are insufficiently prepared and we judge in accordance with our own theories, our habitual ways of thought, and so forth. Just as there is only one correct opinion concerning mathematical problems, so is this also true in accordance with the higher worlds.

But before we may reach such opinions, preparations must first be undertaken by us.

"It is indeed true that these truths and these higher lives live within all our souls, and that each one of us may and must find them for ourselves. But they lie deeply buried and can only be brought up from their deep shafts after all our obstacles have been cleared away."

Only the experienced may advise how this may be done. Such advice is found in Spiritual Science. No truth is forced on anyone; no dogmas are proclaimed, they are only pointed out. It is true that everyone could find their way unaided, but only perhaps after many incarnations. By esoteric training, those ways are shortened. We therefore may reach more quickly points from which we may collaborate with these worlds, and where the salvation and evolution of mankind may be furthered by our spiritual work.

This brings us to the end of the subject of the conditions in our esoteric trainings. The next chapters continue with these connections, and it will be shown how these developments affect the higher elements of our human organisms (the soul-organisms or astral bodies, and the soul-spirits or thought-bodies). In this way, the indications to be given will be placed in a new light, and it will be possible for us to penetrate even deeper.

– Chapter 5 –

SOME RESULTS OF INITIATION

The Need to Study with Full Consciousness

One of the fundamental principles of Spiritual Science is that when we devote ourselves to its study, we should do so with full consciousness. We should never attempt or practice anything without the knowledge of the effects that may be produced. Teachers of Spiritual Science who give advice or instruction will, at the same time, always explain to those striving for higher knowledge the effects that will be produced on our bodies, souls, and spirits, if we are to follow their advice and instructions.

Some of the effects produced upon our souls will be indicated here. We must know such things before we undertake in full consciousness the exercises that lead us to the knowledge of the higher worlds. Without the latter, no genuine esoteric training is possible; and it must be understood that any probing in the dark is discouraged, and that any failure to pursue this training with open eyes may lead us to mediumship, but not to the exact clairvoyance in the sense of Spiritual Science.

The exercises described in the preceding chapters, if we practice them correctly, involve certain changes in our soul organisms (astral bodies). In our astral bodies desires, lusts, passions, and ideas become visible in spiritual ways. The latter are only perceptible to clairvoyants, and may be compared to clouds that are, psycho-spiritually, glowing to a certain degree in the center of our physical bodies.

For instance, those with pure and noble thoughts may find their expressions in a reddish-violet radiance; the clear-cut concepts of logical thinkers may be experienced as yellowish figures with sharply defined outline; the confused thoughts of muddled thinkers may appear as figures with vague outlines. The thoughts of one-sided thinkers may appear sharply outlined but immobile, while the thoughts of people accessible to the points of view of others may be seen to have mobile, changeable outlines. In all these and the following descriptions, it must be noted that by "seeing colors," *spiritual seeing* is meant. For example, when seers speak of "seeing red," they may mean: "We have experiences, in psycho-spiritual ways, which are equivalent to our physical (feelings) experiences when impressions of red are received."

These modes of expression are spoken here because they are perfectly natural for clairvoyants. If these points are overlooked, our mere color-visions may easily be mistaken for our genuine clairvoyant experiences.

The further we advance in our inner development, the more clearly they will be distinguished within our astral bodies. In the case of those with undeveloped inner lives, the latter are confused and undifferentiated. However, clairvoyants can perceive even unorganized astral bodies as figures standing out distinctly from their environments. These astral bodies extend from the center of our heads to the middle of our physical bodies, and appear like independent bodies possessing certain organs.

THE CHAKRAS—SPIRITUAL LOTUS FLOWERS

These organs are perceptible to clairvoyants near the following parts of our physical bodies:

- The first, between our eyes;

- The second, near our throats;

- The third, in the region of our hearts;
- The fourth, in the area of our belly buttons;
- The fifth and sixth, situated in our abdomens.

These organs are technically known as the "sacred wheels," "chakras," or "lotus flowers." They are called these on account of their likeness to wheels or flowers. (In the case of the lotus flower, these expressions must be taken figuratively.)

In undeveloped persons, these lotus flowers (chakras) are dark in color, motionless, and inactive. For clairvoyants, however, they are luminous, mobile, and multi-colored. When we begin these exercises, our chakras will become more luminous; later on, they will begin to spin. We will be unable to perceive the supersensible until we have developed these astral senses.

Thanks to the *chakras* situated in the vicinity of our *throats*, it becomes possible for us to survey clairvoyantly the thoughts and mentalities of other beings, and to obtain deeper insight into the true laws of natural wonder.

The *chakras* situated near our *hearts* permit knowledge of the feelings and natures of other souls. Once developed, these *chakras* also make it possible for us to observe certain deeper forces in animals and plants.

By the means of the *chakras* in our *solar plexus*, the knowledges obtained are of both the gifts and abilities of our souls, and also the parts played by animals, plants, stones, metals, and all the atmospheric wonders of nature.

The *chakras* in the vicinity of our throats have sixteen petals, or spokes; the ones in the region of our hearts, twelve; and the ones at our solar plexus, ten.

Certain activities of our soul are connected with our developing these chakras and devoting ourselves to them in certain definite ways. This also contributes to the development of the other corresponding *chakras*.

Throat Chakra—The 16-Petal Lotus

In our 16-petal chakra (throat chakra), eight of these sixteen petals were developed in our remote pasts, during earlier stages of our human evolutions. We ourselves contributed nothing to these developments; we received them as gifts from nature at a time when our consciousness was still in dull, dream-like states.

At that stage of our human evolution they were actively used, but the manner of these activities was compatible only with our dull states of consciousness.

As our consciousness became clearer and brighter, these petals became obscured and ceased their activities. We ourselves may now develop the remaining eight petals of our throat *chakras* by means of conscious exercises, in which these *chakras* will become luminous and mobile. Our ability to acquire such capabilities depends on the development of each one of our sixteen petals. Yet, as already shown, only eight can be consciously developed; the remainder will appear of their own accord.

In earlier times, eight of the sixteen petals were visible, and the others undeveloped. In future ages, they will all be visible, for the first eight are the results of the actions of unconscious initiations, while the other eight of the conscious initiations are attained by our own personal efforts.

These eight new petals correspond to the Beatitudes of Christ.

> *"All the great Founders of religions*
> *have been possessed of clairvoyant sights.*
> *They are the spiritual Guides of mankind,*
> *and their teachings are teachings of the moral lives*
> *based on astral and spiritual truths.*
> *This explains the similarities in all the religions.*
> *There is a certain similarity, for instance,*
> *between the Eight-fold Path of the Buddha*
> *and the Eight Beatitudes of Christ."*

The same underlying truth is that whenever we develop one of these virtues, we unfold new abilities of perception. Why are eight stages mentioned? Because the seer knows that the capacities which may be transmuted into our organs of perception (chakras) are eight in number (the eighth being our souls).

These developments proceed in the following manner: We must first apply ourselves with care and attention to certain functions of our souls, which we previously exercised in careless and inattentive behaviors.

The Eight Functions in Which Our Ideas and Conceptions Are Acquired

There are eight such soul-functions:
(1) the way in which our ideas and conceptions are acquired;
(2) the control of our resolutions
(3) the control of our speech;
(4) the control of our outward actions;
(5) the management of the whole of life;
(6) the concern with human endeavors;
(7) the concern with learning as much as possible from life; and
(8) the concern with fastidious introspection.

1. The Control of Our Self-Education. We usually allow ourselves to be led by chance alone. We see or hear one thing or another, and form our ideas accordingly. If this is the case, the sixteen petals of our *chakras* will remain ineffective. In the first soul-function, **it is only when we begin to take self-education into our own hands that these petals become effective.** Our ideas and conceptions must be guarded; each single one of our ideas should acquire some forms of significance; and we should express a message of instruction concerning the things of our outer world. We must govern our mental lives so that they become true mirrors of our outer worlds, and direct our efforts to the elimination of any incorrect ideas, empty of any meaning or value.

2. The Control of Our Resolutions. In the second of these functions, **we must not resolve upon even the most insignificant acts without well-founded and thorough consideration.** Thoughtless and meaningless actions should be foreign to our natures. We should have well-considered grounds for everything we do, and abstain from everything for which there is no significant motivation urging us on.

3. The Control of Our Speech. In the third function, **we should utter no words that are devoid of any sense or meaning. All talking for the sake of talking draws us away from our path.** We must avoid the usual kind of conversations and discussions of generally varied topics. This does not imply that we exclude ourselves from interacting with others. We should be ready to converse with everyone, but we should do so thoughtfully and with thorough consideration. We should never speak without grounds for what we say. We must seek to use neither too many nor too few words.

4. The Control of Our Outward Actions. The fourth function is the regulation of our outward actions. **We must try to adjust our actions in such a way that we harmonize with the actions of others as well as the events taking place around us.** We must refrain from any actions which may disturb others around us and/or conflict with our surroundings. We must seek to adjust our actions so that they combine harmoniously with our surroundings and our positions in life. When an external motive causes us to act, we must consider how, as well as the best ways, to respond. We must learn to weigh both the effects and after-effects of our activities.

5. The Management of the Whole of Life. In the fifth function, **we must endeavor to live in conformity with both nature and spirit.** We should never be impulsive or apathetic. Excessive activity and laziness should be equally alien to our being. We should regulate our habits and the care of our health in such a way that they are harmonious.

6. The Concern with Human Endeavors. In the sixth function, **we should test our capacity and proficiency, and**

conduct ourselves in light of the consideration of such self-knowledge. We should attempt nothing beyond our power and omit nothing within our scope. We should aim high towards our ideals and our duties as human beings. We should not regard ourselves as just another existence, but rather seek to comprehend the tasks of our lives and look beyond any trivial limits. We should endeavor to fulfill our obligations ever better and more perfectly.

7. **The Concern with Learning as Much as Possible from Life.** In the seventh function, **nothing should pass before us without giving us occasion to accumulate an experience that would add value in or to our lives.** If we have performed anything wrongly or imperfectly, we should seek the incentive for meeting the same incident later, and performing it both rightly and perfectly. When others act, we should observe them with the same end in mind. We should seek and gather rich stock of our experiences, ever returning to them for further counsel. We should never do anything without first looking back on the experience from which we may derive help in our future decisions and affairs.

8. **The Concern with Fastidious Introspection.** In the eighth function, **we must, from time to time, glance introspectively into ourselves, sink back into ourselves, take counsel within ourselves, form and test the fundamental principles of our lives, run over in our thoughts the sum total of our knowledge, weigh our duties, and reflect upon the content and the aim of our lives.**

All these functions have been mentioned in the preceding chapters. Here, they are merely recapitulated in connection with the development of our sixteen-pedaled lotus (throat *chakra*), which will become ever more perfected by means of these exercises. For it is upon such exercises that the development of our psychic powers depends. The better our thoughts and speech harmonize with the processes in our outer worlds, the more quickly we will develop these abilities.

Whoever thinks and speaks what is contrary to their

truth destroys something in the buds of their sixteen-pedaled lotus (throat *chakra*).

"Truthfulness, uprightness, and honesty are in direct connection to creative forces, while deceptions, deceitfulness, and dishonesty are destructive forces."

We must realize, however, that actual deeds are needed, and not merely good intentions. If we think or say anything that does not conform within our reality, we kill something in our spiritual organs, even though we believed that our intentions were good. The regulations of the above activities of our souls in the manner described causes our sixteen-pedaled lotus (throat *chakra*) to shine in glorious hues, and imparts to it definite movements. Yet it must be noted that these aptitudes of psychic power cannot make their appearance before definite degrees of development of our souls have been reached. **The first traces of psychic powers only appear when we have reached the point of being able to live in specified and habitual ways. The efforts must then no longer be laborious; they must have become matters of course.** There must no longer be a need for us to be continually watching and urging to live in particular ways. These must all have become matters of habit.

The throat *chakra* may be developed in other ways, by following certain other instructions. But all such methods are rejected by true Spiritual Science, for they may lead to the destruction of our physical health and/or lead us toward moral ruin. They are easier to follow than that which has been described here; but though the latter may be prolonged and difficult, only they lead us to our truer goals and strengthen us morally.

Those other, easier-to-follow instructions concerning *chakra* developments, may result not only in those seekers receiving illusions and imaginary conceptions, but—should certain degrees of clairvoyance be obtained—also in errors and instability within their ordinary lives.

It was explained earlier that eight of the sixteen petals of these lotus flowers (*chakras*) were developed in our remote pasts, and that these will re-appear of themselves during our esoteric developments. All efforts and attention must be devoted to the remaining eight. Any of these faulty trainings may easily result in the re-appearance of the earlier petals alone, while the new petals will remain stunted. This will especially ensue if there was any lack of logical and rational thinking, as employed by these trainings. It is of supreme importance that we should always use rational and clear thinking, and it is of further importance that we should always practice clearness of our speech.

At the beginning of our instructions, we may as a rule wonder why our teacher lacked curiosity concerning our experiences. It would be much better for us to remain entirely silent on this subject, and to be contented with mentioning only whether we have been successful or unsuccessful, in our performance and observation of the instructions presented before us. For the teachers have quite other means of estimating our progress than we do ourselves.

"People who begin to have some feeling of the supersensible effects may be apt to shine talkative on these subjects; but by doing, so they will be slowing their normal development. The less we talk about these matters, the better. Only when we have achieved a certain degree of clarity should we speak about them."

The eight petals now under consideration will always become a little hardened through such statements, whereas they should be kept soft and supple.

For the sake of clarity, here is an example based on an ordinary life-experience: Suppose you hear a piece of news and thereupon immediately form an opinion. Shortly afterwards, you receive some further news which does not tally with the previous information. You are thereby obliged to reverse your previous judgment. This result would be an unfavorable influence upon the sixteen-petaled lotus chakra.

Quite the contrary would have been the case if, in the

first place, all judgment was suspended and there remained silence concerning this news—both inwardly in thoughts, and outwardly in words—until there were reliable grounds for forming any kind of judgments.

This caution regarding the formation and pronouncement of our judgment comes to us by degrees, and will be one our most distinctive characteristics. At that time, our receptivity for impressions and experiences will have increased; and we will let them pass over us silently, in order that we may collect and have the largest possible number of facts at our disposal, if the time should come for us to form our opinions.

Please note that similar conditions attached to these developments of the sixteen petals on the lotuses (chakras) were also given by the Buddha to his disciples as instructions for the Path. The same underlying truth is that whenever we develop one of these virtues, we unfold new capacities of perception.

Heart Chakra – The 12-Petal Lotus

The twelve petals on the lotus (*chakra*) situated in the region of our hearts are developed in a similar way. Half their petals, as well, were already existent and inactive for use in those remote stages of our human evolution. Therefore, there are six petals that are not to be developed in our esoteric training; they appear of themselves and begin to evolve when we set to work on the other six. Here again, we learn to promote this development by consciously controlling and directing certain inner activities in special ways.

It must be clearly understood that the perception of each single one of our spiritual organs bears different characteristics. The twelve-lotus flowers (heart *chakra*) and sixteen-petal lotus flowers (throat *chakra*) transmit quite different perceptions. The latter manifests and perceives forms, the thoughts and mentalities of other beings, and the laws governing natural phenomena. The sixteen-petals on the lotus (throat *chakra*) are figures—not rigid motionless figures, but mobile forms filled with life.

Clairvoyants in whom these senses have been developed are able to distinguish them in every mode of their thoughts; for every law of nature, there are forms bearing near impressions. Revengeful thoughts, for example, often assume arrow-like, pronged forms, while our kindly thoughts often are formed like an opening flower, and so on. Clear-cut and significant thoughts are often regular and symmetrical in their forms, while confused thoughts often have wavy outlines.

It also must be noted, in passing, that esoteric training never develops one organ (*chakra*) without also developing the others. The twelve-petal lotus (heart *chakra*), when developed, reveals to clairvoyants deeper understandings of the processes of nature. From the manifestation of growth and development, rays of soul-warmth are delivered, while those contained in the processes of decay, destruction, and ruin present impressions of cold.

The Six Attributes Required of Us

The development of these senses may be furthered in the following manner:

(1) to control our thoughts;
(2) to control our actions;
(3) to cultivate perseverance;
(4) to cultivate tolerance under all circumstances;
(5) to cultivate impartiality to what life brings us, and encounter all living beings with trust;
(6) to cultivate equanimity.

1. We must endeavor to regulate the sequence (control) of our thoughts. Just as the sixteen-petal lotus (throat *chakra*) is developed by the cultivation of thought to conform to truth, so too is the twelve-petal lotus (heart *chakra*) developed by inward control of our trains of thought.

Any thoughts that dart back and forth and that do not follow each other in any logical or rational sequence destroy their forms. The closer our thoughts are made to follow one upon the other, and the more strictly everything of any illogical nature is avoided, the more suitably the forms of these sense organs (*chakras*) develop.

> *"If we hear an illogical thought,*
> *we immediately should let the right*
> *thought pass through our mind instead.*
> *However, we should not withdraw in any*
> *insensitive way from what is perhaps an illogical*
> *environment to further our own development.*
> *Neither should we feel ourselves*
> *compelled to correct all the illogical*
> *thoughts expressed around us.*
> *Rather, we should silently coordinate*
> *our thoughts as they pour in upon us,*
> *and make them conform in a more*
> *logical and sensible way."*

2. **We must have equal consistency in our actions (control of our actions). All inconstancy and all disharmony in our actions are harmful for this lotus (heart** *chakra***).**
"When we perform an action, we must see to it that the action to follow is in the same logical sequence."
If we act from day to day with variable intentions, we will never develop the ability that is measured here.

3. **We must cultivate endurance (perseverance). We must be resistant to any influence which will divert us from the goals we have set out for ourselves, if we regard them as the right goals.** For us, obstacles contain challenges that impel us to overcome them, but are never reasons for giving up.

4. **We must cultivate forbearance (tolerance) toward other persons, creatures, and under all circumstances. We must suppress all unnecessary criticism of all things that**

are imperfect, evil, or bad, and seek rather an understanding towards everything that comes under our notice.

> *"Just as the sun does not withdraw its light*
> *from the bad and the evil, so too must we*
> *not refuse our compassion.*
> *Should some trouble befall us,*
> *we should not proceed to condemn and criticize,*
> *but rather accept that which is inevitable,*
> *and endeavor to the best of our ability to give such*
> *a matter a turn for the best."*

We should not consider the opinions of others merely from our own standpoints, but rather seek to put ourselves into other persons' positions (stand in their shoes).

5. We must cultivate an impartiality toward everything that life brings. In this connection, we speak of our faith and trust. We must encounter every human being and every living creature with our trust, and let them inspire our actions. Upon hearing some information, we should never say: "I don't believe it; it contradicts my present opinion." Rather, we need to be ready to test and rectify, our views and opinions. We must remain receptive to everything that confronts us, and trust in the worthiness of our undertakings. Timidity and skepticism must be banished from our being.

6. We must cultivate inner balance (equanimity). We must endeavor to retain our composure in the face of both joy and sorrow, and eradicate our tendency to fluctuate between that of joy and that of despair. Misfortune and danger, fortune and advancement thus will find us readily armed.

"We must harbor faith in the power of our intentions. A hundred failures cannot rob us of such faith. This is the kind of 'faith which can move mountains.'"

The qualities just described are the Six Attributes required. Special instruction was offered to us in order to bring the lotus flower (heart *chakra*) to fruition; but here, once again, the perfect balance of their form depends on the development of the qualities mentioned.

If we should neglect these attributes, this organ would be formed into a distortion of its proper shape. In such a case, should certain clairvoyance be attained, the quality in question may take an immoral course. We may become intolerant, timid, or contentious toward our environments; for example, we may acquire some feeling towards the attitude of another, and for this very reason shun them or hate them. We may even reach the point where when we hear an offensive opinion, by reason of our inner coldness, we are unable to listen and we behave objectionably.

Our observance of these principles is indispensable. Should we attempt esoteric training without conforming to them, it would only result in our entering the higher worlds with inadequate organs, and instead of perceiving the truth, we would be subject to deceptions and illusions. We would attain a certain clairvoyance but would, for the most part, be the victim of a greater blindness than before.

Formerly, we at the very least stood firmly within our physical world; but now we look beyond our physical world, and grow confused about it before acquiring firm footing into the higher worlds. All power of distinguishing truth from error would perhaps fail us, and we would entirely lose our way. It is for this reason that patience is so necessary in these matters.

It must ever be borne in our mind that the instructions given in this esoteric training may go no further than our willingness and readiness to develop the lotus (chakra) to its regular shape. Should this lotus (chakra) be brought to fruition before it has quietly attained its correct form, a mere caricature would be the result. Maturity may be brought about by the special instructions given in esoteric training, but the form is dependent on the methods described above.

Solar Plexus *Chakra*—The 10-Petal Lotus

Inner training of a particularly intimate nature is necessary for the development of our ten-petal lotus (solar plexus chakra), for it is now a question of our learning how to consciously control and dominate the sense-impressions themselves.

This is of special importance in the initial stages of our clairvoyance, for it is only by these means that sources of countless illusions and fancies may be avoided. People as a rule do not realize what may cause a sudden idea or memory to dominate their thoughts, and how they may be produced.

Consider the following case: You are traveling by railway; your mind is busy with a thought. Suddenly this thought deviates, and you recollect an experience that happened years ago, which interweaves with your present thought. You do not notice, when looking out through the window, that you caught sight of a person who resembled another person who is intimately connected with this recollected experience. You remain conscious not of what you saw, but rather of the effect that was produced—and thus you believe that it all came to you of your own accord. How much in our lives occurs in such a way!

How great are the parts played in our lives by things we hear and learn, without our consciously realizing the connections! Say that you, for instance, cannot bear a certain color; but you do not realize that this is due to the fact that one of your school teachers, whom you used to worry over many years ago, wore a coat with the same color. Innumerable illusions are based upon such associations.

Many things leave a mark upon our soul while remaining outside the pale of our consciousness. For example: you read in the paper about the death of a well-known person, and immediately claim to have had a premonition of this the day before, although you had neither heard nor seen anything that might have given rise to such a thought. However, it seems quite clear to you that this thought occurred to you yesterday, as though of your own accord, that this particular person would die.

Only one thing escaped your attention: two or three hours before the thought occurred to you yesterday, you went to visit a friend. A newspaper lay on the table; you did not actually read it, but your eyes unconsciously fell on the announcement that this particular person in question was very ill. You remain unconscious of this impression you had received, and yet this impression resulted in your premonition of the death.

Reflecting upon this matter shows how great is the source of illusion and fantasy contained in such an association. It is just the source which must be blocked by all who seek to develop their ten-petal lotus (solar plexus chakra). The truth depends on the attainment of our immunity from the above-mentioned illusion. For this purpose, it is necessary that we should control and dominate everything that seeks to influence us from the outside.

We should reach the point of really receiving no impressions beyond those we wish to receive. This may only be achieved by developing powerful inner lives; by the effort of our own wills, we must only allow such things to impress on us to which our attention is directed, and we should avoid all impressions to which we do not voluntarily want to respond.

This means that if we see something, it is because we will to see it; and if we do not voluntarily take notice of something, it is non-existent to us. The greater our energy and inner activity are devoted to this activity, the more extensively the capability will be attained.

"We must avoid all vacant gazing
and mechanical listening.
For us, the only thing that exists is
what we choose to turn our
eyes or our ears to."

We must practice the power of hearing nothing, even in the greatest of disturbances, if we do not will to hear it. And we must make our eyes unimpressionable to things of which we do not particularly want to take notice. We must be shielded as if by inner armor against all unconscious impressions.

In these connections, we must devote special care to our thought-lives. These thoughts must be singled out. We must endeavor to link them with only such other thoughts as we may ourselves consciously and voluntarily produce.

> *"We must reject all casual ideas and not connect these thoughts with others until we have investigated the origins of the latter."*

We go still further. If, for instance, you may feel a particular dislike for something, you must combat this feeling, and endeavor to establish a conscious relationship between yourself and this particular something in question. In this way, the unconscious elements that intrude into your soul will become fewer and fewer. Only by such severe self-discipline can the ten-petal lotus (solar plexus chakra) attain its proper form.

> *"Our inner lives must become lives of attention, and we must learn to hold at a distance everything to which we should not, or do not wish to, direct our attention."*

If this strict self-discipline is accompanied by meditation, as prescribed in our esoteric training, the lotus (solar plexus chakra) in the region of our stomach will come to maturity in the right way, and lights and colors of a spiritual kind will now be added to their form with warmth.

Sacral Chakra – 6-Petal Lotus

Still greater difficulty appears in the development of the six-petal lotus situated in the center of our body (sacral *chakra*). **This is only achieved as the result of our complete mastery and control over our own personality through the consciousness of our own self, so that our body, soul, and spirit form into one harmonious whole. The function of our body, the inclinations and passions of our soul, and the thoughts and ideas of our spirit must be tuned into perfect harmony.**

Our body must be so cleansed and purified, that our organ incites to nothing that is not of service to our soul and spirit. Our soul must not be compelled through our body toward any kind of lusts or passion that are incompatible with pure and noble thoughts.

Yet our spirit must not stand like a slave driver over our soul, dominating it through laws and commandments. Our souls must learn to obey these laws and duties out of our own free inclinations. We must not feel that our duties are oppressive powers to which we must unwillingly submit, but rather something which we perform out of love.

Our souls must learn to obey these laws and duties out of our own free inclinations. We must not feel that our duties are oppressive powers to which we must unwillingly submit, but rather something which we perform out of love.

The 6-petal lotus, once developed, permits our communication with the beings of higher worlds, though only when their existence is manifested in our astral or soul-worlds. Developing this Lotus (sacral *chakra*) is not advisable unless we have made great progress on the path of our esoteric development which enables us to raise our spirits into still higher worlds.

"Our task is to develop a free soul that maintains equilibrium between our body and spirit. We are no longer required to curb our passions, as of our own accord we are following that which is good."

"Our proper entry into the spiritual worlds must always run parallel with the development of our lotuses (chakras), otherwise we will fall into error and confusion. We would undoubtedly be able to see, but we would remain incapable of forming a correct estimate of what we are actually seeing."

The development of the six-petal lotus (sacral *chakra*) itself provides us certain security against any kinds of confusion or instability, for we are not easily confused once we have attained perfect equilibrium among our senses (our bodies), passions (our souls), and ideas (our spirits). Living beings of an independent existence are revealed to us in spirit, beings belonging to worlds completely different from the world known to our physical senses.

The development of our six-petal lotus (sacral *chakra*) alone will not assure us sufficient security in the higher worlds; still higher organs are necessary. The latter will now be described before the remaining lotus (*chakra*) and the further organization of our soul-body is discussed. (The expression "soul-body"—although obviously contradictory, if taken literally— is used because, to intuitive perception, the impression received spiritually corresponds to the same impression perceived when viewing our physical body.)

Hearing the Inner Worlds

The development of our soul-body permits our perception of the supersensible worlds; but if we wish to find our way in these worlds, we must not remain stationary at this stage of development. The mere movement of the lotuses (chakras) is not sufficient in and of themselves. **We must acquire the power of regulating and controlling these energy flows independently, and with complete consciousness.** Otherwise, we would become mere playthings for the external forces and powers.

To avoid this, we must acquire the ability of hearing what is called the inner worlds, and this involves the development of not only our soul-bodies but also our etheric bodies. The latter are the vague bodies revealed to seers as a kind of double of our physical bodies, and form to a certain extent an intermediate step between our soul nature and our physical body.

It is possible for those equipped with divine power to consciously suggest away the physical bodies of people beyond what is there. If they exert this ability in the case of some person standing before them, there remains visible to their sight only the etheric body, in addition to the soul-body. The soul bodies are larger than the etheric and physical bodies, and interpenetrate them both. Our etheric body has approximately the size and form of our physical body, so that these bodies practically fill the same space. They are extremely delicate and finely organized structures. Their ground-colors are different from any of the seven colors contained in the rainbow.

The particles of our etheric bodies are in continual motion. Countless currents stream through them in all directions. By these currents, our lives themselves are maintained and regulated. Every living being, including animals and plants, possesses etheric bodies. Even in minerals, traces may be observed.

These currents and movements are, to begin with, independent of human will and consciousness, just as the actions of our hearts or stomachs are beyond our control. A certain stage in development consists precisely in adding to our unconscious the currents and movements of our etheric bodies, which must be consciously produced and controlled.

"When our esoteric development has progressed
so far that our lotus (chakra) flowers
begin to stir, much has been achieved.
This results in the formation of certain quite definite
currents and movements in our etheric bodies.

> *The object of their development is the formation in the center region of our physical heart, which radiates currents and movements in the greatest possible variety of colors and forms."*

These centers are not mere points, but most complicated structures and most wonderful organs. They glow and shimmer with all shades of colors and display forms of great symmetry, capable of rapid transformation. Other forms and streams of colors radiate from these organs to the other parts of our body, and beyond them to our astral body, completely penetrating and illuminating it.

> *"The most important of these currents flows to our lotuses (chakras). They permeate each petal and regulate their revolutions; then, streaming out at the points of the petals, they lose themselves in outer space. The higher our development, the greater the circumference to which these rays extend."*

The twelve-petal lotus (heart *chakra*) has a particularly close connection with our central organ (our heart). The currents flow directly into them and through them, proceeding on the one side to the sixteen-petal lotus (throat *chakra*) and the two-petal lotus (third-eye chakra); and on the other, the lower side, to the lotuses of ten petals (solar plexus *chakra*), six petals (sacral chakra) and four petals (root *chakra*).

It is for this reason that the very greatest care must be devoted to the development of the twelve-petal lotus (heart *chakra*), for any imperfection in the latter would result in irregular formations of our entire structure.

All this gives an idea of the delicate and intimate nature of our esoteric training , and of the accuracy needed if this development is to be regular and correct. If we follow the directions that have been provided, we introduce into our etheric body currents and movements which harmonize with the laws and the evolutions of the world to which we belong.

Reflections of the Great Laws of Cosmic Evolution

Consequently, these instructions are reflections of the great laws of cosmic evolution. They consist of the above-mentioned, and similar exercises in our meditation and concentration—which, if correctly practiced, produce the results described. We must at certain times let these instructions permeate our souls with their content, so that we are inwardly, outwardly, and entirely filled with them.

A simple start can be made with viewing and then deepening the logical activities in our minds, and then producing the inward strengthening of our thoughts. Our thoughts are thereby made free and independent of all our other sense impressions and experiences; they are concentrated in and held entirely under our control at this point. Thus, the preliminary center is formed for the currents of our etheric body.

These centers are not as yet in the region of our heart, but in that of our head; and this appears to a clairvoyant as the point of departure for movements and currents. No esoteric training can be successful which does not first create this center. If the latter were first formed in the region of our heart, an aspiring seer would doubtlessly obtain glimpses of the higher worlds, but would lack all true insight into the connection between these higher worlds and the world of the senses. These, however, are an unconditional necessity for mankind at our present stage of evolution. A Seer must not become a visionary; the Seer must retain firm footing upon the earth.

Attention on the center in our head, once duly fixed, is then moved lower downward, to the region of the larynx. This is affected by further exercise in concentration. Then the currents of the etheric body radiate from this point and illuminate the astral spaces surrounding it.

Continued practice enables us to determine for ourselves the position of our etheric bodies. Previously, these positions depended upon external forces proceeding from our physical bodies. Through further development, we will be able to turn our etheric bodies to all sides. This ability is affected by currents moving approximately along both our hands, and centered in our two-petal lotus (third-eye *chakra*) in the region of our eyes. All these are made possible through the radiation from our larynx assuming round forms, of which a number flow to the two-petal lotus (third-eye *chakra*), and from there form rippling currents along the hands.

As a further development, these currents branch out and subdivide in the most delicate of manners and become, as it were, a kind of web which then encompasses our entire etheric bodies as though within networks. Whereas previously our etheric bodies were not closed to the outer worlds, so that our life currents from the universal oceans of life flowed freely in and out, now these currents must pass through these membranes. Thus, we become sensitive to these external streams; and they become perceptible to us.

We Become Gifted with the Inner Worlds

And now the time has come to point to the complete system of currents and movements at their center, which is situated in the region of the heart. **This is again affected through the use of concentration and meditation; and at this point, the stage has been reached when we become gifted with inner worlds. All things now acquire new significance. They become, as it were, spiritually audible in our inner selves, and speak to us of their essential beings.** The currents described above place us in touch with the inner beings of the world to which we belong. We begin to mingle our lives with the lives of our environments and can let them resonate in the movements of our lotus flowers (*chakras*).

At this point, the spiritual worlds have entered. If we have advanced thus far, we acquire a new understanding for all that of which the great teachers of humanity have spoken. The sayings of the Buddha and the Gospels, for instance, produce new effects on us. They pervade us with raptures of which we had never dreamed of before. For the tones of their words follow the movements and rhythms which we ourselves, have formed within ourselves.

> *"We now have gained positive knowledge that Buddha or the Evangelists did not utter their own revelations, but rather that those which flowed into them were from those of the innermost beings of all things."*

A fact must be pointed out which can only be understood in the light of what has been said above: The many sayings of the Buddha are not comprehensible to people of our present evolutionary stage. For us, however, they become a force on which we gladly let our inner senses rest, for they correspond with certain movements in our etheric bodies. Devotionally, we surrender to them with perfect inner peace, and create inner harmony within these movements. And because the latter are images of certain cosmic rhythms—which also, at certain points, repeat themselves and revert to former modes—our listening to the wisdom of the Buddha unites our lives with that of the cosmic mysteries.

THE FOUR ATTRIBUTES MUST BE INCORPORATED INTO OUR SOULS

> *"In esoteric training, there are four attributes which must be acquired on the so-called preparatory path for the attainment of higher knowledge: (1) the ability to discriminate between truth and mere opinion; (2) the ability to correctly estimate what is inwardly true vs. what is apparent; (3) the ability to control our thoughts and actions, perseverance, tolerance, faith, and equanimity; and (4) the love of inner freedom."*

The first attribute is **the ability to discriminate in our thoughts between the truth or mere opinion.** The second attribute is **the correct estimation of what is inwardly true**

and real, against what is merely apparent. The third attribute rests in **the practice of the six qualities** already mentioned in the previous pages: thought-control, control of our actions, perseverance, tolerance, faith, and equanimity. The fourth attribute is **the love of inner freedom.**

Consider, for instance, the first of these attributes: **the discrimination between truth and appearance.**

"We must train ourselves, as a matter of course, to distinguish in everything that confronts us between those elements which are non-essential, and those which are significant and essential."

We will only succeed in this through our own observation of the outer world, and we must quietly and patiently, ever and again repeat our attempts. The end result is that we will be able to naturally single out what is essential at a glance, whereas formerly we would have been contented with the non-essential, and the short-lived, too. All that is transient (passing) is but a seeming truth; and our truths become an unquestionable conviction of our souls. The same applies to the remaining three of the four attributes mentioned above.

Now these four inner attributes have, through using our habits, produced a transformation of our delicate human etheric bodies. First, we are able to discriminate between truth and appearances; the center in our heads are formed, and the center in the region of our larynxes are prepared. The actual development of these centers are of course dependent on our having concentrated and completed the exercises described previously. If we acquire the ability of estimation (assessment), the facts of the higher worlds will gradually become perceptible to us.

"Even the most insignificant of actions, every little thing accomplished, has something of importance in the great cosmic picture, and it is merely a question of being aware of them. Correct estimation (assessment) of our daily affairs is required, not an underestimation of them."

The six virtues of which the third attribute consists have already been dealt with; they are connected with the development of our twelve-petal lotus (heart *chakra*) in the region of our heart; and, as already indicated, they are the center towards which the life-currents of our etheric body must be directed. The fourth attribute, the longing for liberation, serves to bring to fruition the etheric organs in our heart region.

Once these attributes become inner habits, we free ourselves from everything which depends upon the capacity of our own personal nature. We cease to view things from our own separate standpoints, and all our narrow and limited points of view disappear. The secrets of the spiritual world gain access to our inner being. We are liberated. For those restrictions constrained us to thinking that all things and beings corresponded only to our own personal traits.

The instructions given in these esoteric trainings exert the determining influence concerning reaching the innermost depths of human nature. They can be found in one form or another in all the great branches of the Spiritual Sciences that deal with the universe, and that take account of the spiritual worlds.

The Founders/Initiates of the Great Cosmogonies

The founders did not give mankind their teachings from some vague feelings; they gave them for the good reason that they were great initiates. Out of their knowledge, they shaped their moral teachings. They knew how these moral teachings would act upon the finer natures of mankind, and desired that their followers should gradually achieve the developments of these finer natures.

To live in the sense of these great sciences means to work for the attainment of our personal spiritual perfection. Only by so doing will we become servants of the world and of all of humanity.

> *"Self-perfection is by no means self-seeking, for we, as imperfect beings, are imperfect servants of the world and of humanity. The more perfect we become, the better do we serve the world. "If the rose adorns itself, it also adorns the garden."'*

The founders of the great cosmogonies are therefore the great initiates. Their teachings flow into our souls, and thus, through humanity, the whole world moves forward. Quite consciously, they worked to further the evolutionary process of humanity. Their teachings can only be understood by our remembering that they are the products of knowledge of the innermost depths of human nature.

> *"The great initiates knew, and it is out of their knowledge that they shaped the ideals of humanity. We approach the level of these great leaders when we uplift our own selves, in our own developments, to their heights."*

Completely new lives open up before us when the development of our etheric bodies are activated as described previously; and at the proper time in the course of our training, we will receive the enlightenment which will enable us to adapt ourselves to this new existence.

Spiritual Figures and the Throat Chakra 16-Petal Lotus

Our sixteen-petal lotus (throat *chakra*) enables us to perceive spiritual figures of the higher worlds. We must now learn how these different spiritual figures may be produced in different objects or beings.

First, we must notice that our own thoughts and feelings exert a powerful influence on certain figures, and yet on others offer little or no influence at all. One kind of figure alters immediately upon seeing them, and we may say to ourselves: "This is beautiful," and then in the course of the same observation we change our thought to: "This is useful."

These figures, too, are full of life and motion. However, the motions are only partially due to the influence of our thoughts and feelings; they are produced by causes which are beyond our influence. Now, there appears within this entire world a species which remains almost entirely unaffected by human influence.

We may convince ourselves that these forms progress neither from minerals nor from artificial objects nor, again, from plants or animals. To gain a complete understanding, we must study these forms which we realize may have progressed from our own feelings, instincts, and passions, if only by a relatively small extent.

But there always remain residues of forms in this world, upon which such influences are negligible. Indeed, at the outset of these aptitudes we may perceive little beyond these residues. We can only discover their natures by observing ourselves. We then learn what forms we ourselves produce from our own wills, our wishes, and so on, and which are expressed in these forms.

Instincts that dwell within us, desires that fill us, intentions that we harbor, and so forth, are all manifested in these forms: our entire characters display themselves in these worlds of forms. Thus, by our own conscious thoughts and feelings, we are able to exercise and have influence over not only all forms which do not progress from ourselves, but also over those which we bring about in the higher worlds, once we have created them.

Now, it follows from what has been said that on these higher planes, our inner instincts, desires, and ideas display themselves outwardly in definite forms, just like all the other beings and objects. To higher knowledge, these inner worlds appear as part of the outer worlds. In higher worlds, our inner beings confront us as reflected images, just as though in the physical world we were surrounded by mirrors and could observe our physical body in these same ways.

At this stage of our development we have reached the point where we may free ourselves from the illusions resulting from the initiations of our personal selves. Our sixteen-petal lotus (throat *chakra*) invites and allows an authentic expression of our inner worlds, first towards ourselves, then towards the outside world. In this way, we have purified our expressions until we are able to fully live as our true selves, with a free flow between the outer and inner worlds.

Thus, we learned by gradual experience to deal with ourselves as previously we dealt with the beings around us. Were we to obtain such an insight into the spiritual worlds without sufficient preparation regarding our true nature, we would have found ourselves confronted by the picture of our own souls as though unknown.

Now, upon entering these worlds, entirely new methods of judgment must be acquired; for apart from the fact that things actually pertaining to our inner natures appear as outer worlds, they also bear the characters of mirrored reflections of what they really are. When, for instance, a number is perceived, it must be read in reverse, as a picture in a mirror: 265 would mean here, in reality, 562. A sphere is perceived as thought from its center.

Inner Perception

Inner perception must be translated in the correct way. The quality of our souls appear as if in mirrors. Wishes directed toward outer objects appear as forms moving towards us. Passions residing in the lower part of our human natures may assume animal forms or similar shapes that hurl against us. In reality, these passions are headed outward; they seek satisfaction in the outer worlds, but their striving outward appears in the mirrored reflection as an attack on us.

> *"If our insights into the higher worlds are
> earned by quiet and sincere self-observation,
> and we realize the qualities and the defects
> of our own characters,
> at these moments when our own inner selves
> confront ourselves as mirrored images,
> we will then find strength and courage to
> conduct ourselves in the right way."*

Those who have failed to test themselves in such ways, and are insufficiently acquainted with their own inner selves will not recognize themselves in their own mirrored images, and will mistake these images for alien realities. Or they may become alarmed at these visions and — because they cannot endure these sights — deceive themselves into believing that the entire matter is nothing but an illusion which cannot lead them anywhere. In either of these cases, those in question, through attaining certain stages of their inner development prematurely, will fatally obstruct their own progress.

> *"It is necessary that
> we should experience
> the spiritual aspects of
> our own inner selves
> before progressing to
> higher spheres; for our
> own selves constitute
> the psycho-spiritual
> elements of which we
> are the best judge."*

Having thoroughly realized the nature of our own personalities in the physical world, if these images of our personalities first appeared to us in the higher worlds, we would be able to compare them with each other. We would refer the higher to something already known to us so that, at the point of our departures, we will stand on firm ground.

No matter how many other spiritual beings appeared to us, we would find ourselves unable to discover their true natures and qualities, and would soon feel the ground giving way beneath us. **It cannot be emphasized enough that the only safe entrance into the higher worlds is,** at the end, paths leading through our genuine knowledge and assessment of our own inner natures.

Pictures, now of a spiritual kind, are first encountered in our progression into higher worlds; and the reality to which these pictures correspond is within ourselves. We will soon meet something quite new within this world of pictures. Our lower selves are before us as mirrored images, but from within these images appear the true realities of our higher selves.

THE SIGNIFICANCE OF OUR THIRD-EYE LOTUS (CHAKRA)

Out of these pictures of our lower personalities, the forms of our spiritual egos become visible. Then the threads are spun from our spiritual egos to our lower personalities which lead us to a higher spiritual reality. This is the moment when the two-petal lotus (third-eye *chakra*) in the region of our eyes is required. If it now begins stirring, we will find it possible to bring our higher egos in contact with higher spiritual beings.

The currents that flow from this lotus flower (third-eye *chakra*) flow towards our higher realities in a way so that their movement becomes fully apparent. Just as the light renders the physical objects visible, so, too, these currents disclose spiritual beings of higher worlds. They are believed to represent the last remaining dualities: that of our selves and God.

In our third-eye *chakra*, we realize our true selves as souls; but we have still not merged into total unity with God Itself. It is at this stage of our development that the value of our sound judgment, and training with clear and logical thoughts come to the fore.

OUR HIGHER SELVES

Our higher selves, which had before slumbered unconsciously in an embryonic state, are now born into conscious existence. These are not figurative but positive births in the spiritual worlds; and in being born, our higher selves must enter these worlds with all the necessary organs and aptitudes capable of living. Just as nature provides for children being born into the world with suitable eyes and ears, so too are the laws of our self-development that must provide for the necessary capacities with which our higher selves may enter their existence.

> *"Our spiritual selves mature as*
> *our physical selves did*
> *within our mothers' wombs.*
> *A child's health depends upon*
> *the normal functioning of natural laws*
> *in the maternal womb.*
> *The constitution of our spiritual selves*
> *are similarly conditioned."*

We are unable to birth our soundly constituted higher selves when the lives of our thoughts and feelings in the physical world are not sound and healthy. A **natural, rational life is the basis of all genuine spiritual development. Just as children, out of their dim life-instincts, acquire the requisite forces, so too do we acquire the powers of the spiritual worlds before our higher selves are born.**

Certainly, we must do this if the latter are to enter the world as fully developed beings. It would be wrong for us to say: "We cannot accept the teachings of the Spiritual Sciences until we ourselves are seers," for without inward application and the results of our spiritual research there is no chance whatsoever of attaining genuine higher knowledge. It would be as though children, during their gestation, were to refuse the forces coming to them through their mothers and proposed to wait until they could procure them for themselves.

Just as embryonic children, in their developing feelings for life, learn to appreciate what is offered to them, so can the non-seer appreciate the truth of the teachings of the Spiritual Sciences. Insight into these teachings are based on deeply

SOME RESULTS OF INITIATION

rooted feelings for the truth.

We are now able to distinguish the imperishable in ourselves from the perishable; that is, we have learned through our own personal insights to understand the doctrine of the incarnation of our higher selves into that of the lower. It becomes clear to us that we are part of a greater spiritual complex, and that our qualities and destinies are due to these connections.

> *"We now have direct knowledge of our higher selves. We learn how our higher selves are connected to exalted spiritual beings, and how we form with them a united whole."*

We learn to recognize the laws of our lives as our *karmas*. We realize that our lower selves constitute our present existence, and are only one of the forms which our higher beings will adopt. We discern the possibility of working down from our higher selves into our lower selves, so that we may perfect ourselves ever more.

We are now able to comprehend the greater differences between human beings in regard to their levels of perfection. We become aware that there are others above us who have already traversed these stages which still lie before us, and we realize that these teachings and the deeds of such people proceed from the inspirations of higher worlds.

We know that this knowledge being offered is our first personal glimpse into the higher worlds. These, then, are the gifts which we are indebted toward for our developments at this stage:

1. Insight into our higher selves.
2. Insight into the doctrines of the incarnations of our higher beings into our lower.
3. Insight into the laws by which our lives in the physical world are regulated according to our spiritual connections—that is, the laws of karma.
4. Insight into the existence of all the great initiates.

Thus, it is said that for those who have reached this stage, all doubts have vanished. Former faiths, based on reasoning and sound thoughts, are now replaced by knowledge and insights which nothing may weaken. The various religions have presented, in their ceremonies, sacraments, and rites, externally visible patterns of the higher spiritual beings and events. None but those who have not penetrated to the depths of these great religions can fail to recognize these as facts.

Our personal own insights into our spiritual realities explain the great significance of these externally visible worships.

> *"Religious services, then,*
> *become for those who are visionaries*
> *as images of their own communion with*
> *the higher spiritual worlds.*
> *It has been shown how, by attaining this stage,*
> *we become, in truth, new beings."*

We may now mature to still higher capabilities and — by means of the life-currents of our etheric bodies — control our higher and actual life-elements, thus attaining higher degrees of independence from the restrictions of our physical bodies.

– CHAPTER 6 –

THE TRANSFORMATION OF DREAM LIFE

The changes that come to us in our dream lives are indications that we have reached, or will soon reach, the stage of development described in the preceding chapter.

That is, our dreams (which previously were confusing and haphazard) now begin to assume a more regular character. Their pictures begin to succeed each other in sensible connections, through the thoughts and ideas found in our daily lives. We can discern in them laws, causes, and effects.

The *contents* of our dreams have changed, as well. While previously we discerned only a reminiscence of our daily life and transformed impressions of the surroundings of our physical conditions, there now appear before us pictures of worlds we previously had not known.

At first, the general character of our dream life remains unchanged, in as far as our dreams are distinguished from our waking mental activities and by the symbolic presentations of that which wishes to be expressed.

No attentive observers of dream life can fail to detect these characteristics. For instance, we may dream that we have caught some horrible creature, and start to feel an unpleasant sensation in our hands. We wake to discover that we are tightly grasping the corners of our blankets. This truth is not presented to our mind, except through the medium of these metaphorical (symbolic) images.

We may dream that we are flying away from some pursuer, and we are stricken with fear. Upon our waking, we find that we had been suffering, during our sleep, from palpitations of the heart. Disquieting dreams can also be traced to indigestible food.

Occurrences in our immediate vicinity may also reflect themselves symbolically in our dreams. For example, a falling chair may be the occasion of a whole dream drama in which the sound of the fall is reproduced as that of a gun, and so forth. **Our dreams will become more regulated as our etheric bodies continue to develop.** We will still retain the metaphorical methods of expression, but we will cease redirecting those realities connected with our physical bodies and physical environments. **As our dreams become more connected, they are mingled with similar pictures expressing things and events of other worlds.** These are the first experiences lying beyond the range of our waking consciousness.

Yet no true seer will ever make these experiences in dreams the basis of any authoritative account of the higher worlds. Such dreams must be merely considered as providing the first hints of our higher development.

Hereafter, in the far future, we will be mentally controlled and supervised as with the impressions and conceptions of our waking consciousness. The difference between dreaming and waking consciousness will grow ever smaller. As dreamers, we will remain awake in the fullest sense of the word during our dream life: that is, fully aware of our mastery and control over our own vivid mental activities.

During our dreams, we are actually in worlds other than that of our own physical sense-world; but with our undeveloped spiritual organs, we form only confused conceptions of those worlds. Presently, for instance, the world of our senses is equipped with no more than undeveloped eyes. The latter are perceptible to us because our own souls paint our daily experiences in pictorial forms into the substances of which the other worlds consist.

> *"It must be clearly understood that in addition to our ordinary conscious workaday life, we lead a second, unconscious life in other worlds."*

We inscribe it all in our thoughts and perceptions. These tracings may only become visible when our lotus petals (*chakras*) are developed.

In all human beings there are slender rudiments of these lotus petals (*chakras*). We are unable to perceive them during our waking consciousness because the impressions made on them are very faint. We cannot see the stars during the daytime for similar reasons: their visibility is extinguished by the mighty glare of the sun. Thus, too, the faint spiritual impressions cannot make themselves felt in the face of the powerful impressions received through our senses.

When the gates of our senses are closed during sleep, other impressions begin to emerge, and we, the dreamers, become aware of experiences in other worlds. But as already explained, these experiences consist at first merely of pictures engraved in the spiritual worlds by the mental activity attached to our physical senses. Only developed lotuses (*chakras*) make it possible for manifestations not derived from our physical worlds to be imprinted in the same way. Our etheric bodies, once developed, will bring forth full knowledge concerning these engraved impressions derived from these other worlds.

This is the beginning of our life and activity in new worlds; and at this point in our esoteric training we must set ourselves a two-fold task. To begin with, we must learn to take stock of everything we observe in our dreams, exactly as though we were awake. Then, if we are successful in this, we are led to make the same observations during our ordinary waking consciousness.

In doing so, we will train our attention and receptivity for these spiritual impressions so that they no longer vanish in the face of our physical impressions, but they will always be at hand and will reach for us.

Once we have acquired this ability, there arises before our spiritual eyes something of the pictures described in the former chapter; and we now distinguish all that the spiritual worlds contain are but the causes of our physical worlds.

Knowledge of Our Higher Self and Higher Consciousness

Above all things, we may perceive and gain knowledge of our own higher selves.

The next task now confronting us is to grow, as it were, into our higher selves—that is, really to regard them as our own true selves and act accordingly. We adopt the attitude toward our lower self as being limited to the world of our senses, and we adopt our senses as instruments or vehicles that serve us and humanity. We do not include as part of ourselves the vehicles in which we are traveling, even though we may say: "I travel." So too, when—as inwardly developed beings—we would say, "I go through the door," our actual conception is, "*I carry my body through the door.*"

"We now realize ever more clearly and intensely that our physical bodies and what we previously called our "I" are merely the instruments of our higher selves."

We must develop this as a natural concept, so that we never for a moment lose our firm footing in our physical world, or feel estranged from it. In order to avoid becoming a whimsical visionary, we must not impoverish our life through our higher consciousness but on the contrary enrich it, such as we enrich our life by using our car and not merely our legs to travel to places.

Once we have raised ourselves to our life in our higher ego—or rather, during our acquisition of our higher consciousness—then we learn how to stir to life the spiritual perceptive forces in the organ of our heart and control them through the currents described in the former chapter. These perceptive forces are elements of higher sustainability, which proceed from our organs in question and flow with beautiful radiance through the moving lotuses (*chakras*) and the other channels of our developed etheric bodies.

From there, they radiate outward into the surrounding spiritual worlds, rendering them spiritually visible, just as sunlight falling on the objects of the physical world renders them visible. How these perceptive forces in our heart organ are created only gradually may be understood in the course of our actual development.

It is only when these organs of perception are able to be sent through our etheric body out into the outer worlds in order to light up the objects there that the actual spiritual worlds which are composed of objects and beings may be clearly perceived.

*"Our complete consciousness of these objects
in spiritual worlds is only made possible when
we ourselves cast our spiritual lights upon them.
Now our egos, which create these organs of perception,
do not dwell within us but rather outside us
and our physical body."*

Our heart organ is the only spot from where we ignite without these spiritual-light organs. Were they concluded and ignited elsewhere, the spiritual perceptions produced by them would have no connection with our physical world.

*"All our higher spiritual realities must be related
to our physical world, and we must ourselves act
as channels through which they flow into.
It is precisely through our heart organ that our
higher egos govern our physical selves,
making us their instruments."*

The feelings of esoterically developed beings towards their belonging in spiritual worlds are vastly different from the feelings of undeveloped beings toward their belonging in their physical world. The latter feel themselves in the world of their senses, and all surrounding objects are perceived by them to be external. As spiritually developed beings, however, we feel ourselves to be united with, and in the center of, the spiritual objects which we perceive.

Spiritually developed beings wander from place to place in spiritual space, and are therefore called the wanderers in the language of the occult sciences. We have no home, at first. Should we, however, remain mere wanderers, we would be unable to define any objects in our spiritual space. Just as objects and places in our physical space are defined from fixed points of departure, this is also the case in the other worlds.

We must seek out our place, thoroughly investigate it, and take spiritual possession of it. In this place, we must establish our spiritual home and relate everything else to it. In our physical life, as well, we must see everything in terms of our physical home.

Yet there are differences between our spiritual home and our physical home. We are born into our physical home without our co-operation, and during our childhood we instinctively absorb several ideas by which everything is involuntarily colored from that time on. However, we have found our own *spiritual* home through ourselves, in full consciousness. Therefore, our judgment based on our spiritual home is formed in the light of this freedom. The founding of our spiritual home, in the language of the occult sciences, is called *the building of the hut*.

Our spiritual vision at this stage extends to the spiritual counterpart of our physical world, so far as it exists in our so-called astral world. There, too, everything found in nature is like our human instincts, feelings, desires, and passions. For the powers related to all these human characteristics are also associated with all physical objects.

Crystals, for instance, are cast in their forms by powers which are seen from a higher standpoint. Similar forces drive the sap through the capillaries of plants, causing their blossoms to unfold, and the seeds are the vessels to their eruptions. To developed spiritual organs of perception, all these forces appear gifted with forms and colors, just as the objects of our physical world have forms and colors for our physical eyes.

At this stage in our development, we see not only the crystals and the plants, but also animal and human impulses are perceptible to us—not only through their physical manifestations, but also directly as spiritual objects. These whole ranges of instincts, impulses, desires, and passions—both of animals and of human beings—constitute the astral clouds or auras in which all beings are enveloped.

Seers at this stage are able to perceive things which, at one time, were fully or almost entirely withheld from their senses. They can, for instance, tell the astral differences between a room full of low-minded or high-minded people. Not only the physical atmospheres, but also the spiritual atmospheres—for example, how hospitals differ from ballrooms. Commercial towns have different astral airs from those of university towns.

In the initial stages of our divining, these perceptive capabilities are only slightly developed; our relationships to the objects in question are similar to the relationships with our dream consciousness and with our waking consciousness in our ordinary lives. They will, however, become fully awakened at this stage, as well.

The highest achievement, once we have attained this degree of vision, are the astral counterparts of our impulses and our passions. Loving actions are accompanied by quite different astral counterparts than are those inspired by hate. Senseless desires give rise to ugly astral counterparts, while feelings evoked by high ideals create ones that are beautiful. These astral images are but faintly perceptible during our physical lives, because their strength is diminished in our physical world.

Our desire for an object, for example, produces a counterpart to the likeness of that desire itself in the astral worlds. If, however, this object is attained and the desire satisfied—or if, at any rate, the possibility of the satisfaction is forthcoming—the corresponding image will show only faintly. This is only attained again in full force after our death, when our soul, in accordance with its nature, still harbors such a desire but is no longer able to be satisfied because the object and our physical organs are both missing. Gourmets, for example, will still retain after their deaths the desire to please their palates; but there is no possibility of their satisfying this desire because they no longer have palates. As a result, these desires produce especially powerful counterparts, and our souls remain tormented. They only vanish when our souls have purified themselves from all the desires influenced by our physical worlds. It is only then that our souls move to the higher regions, to the worlds of spirits.

Even though these images are faint during our lives in the physical world, they are ever present—following us as our world of desire—in the way that comets are followed by their tails. These and similar experiences fill our lives. However, we cannot attain higher spiritual experiences at this stage in our development. We must still climb higher.

– CHAPTER 7 –

THE CONTINUITY OF CONSCIOUSNESS

Our lives run through the course of three alternating states and conditions—specifically: waking, dreaming sleep, and dreamless sleep. Our attainment of higher knowledge of the spiritual worlds can be understood beginning with our understanding of the changes that occur during these three conditions. If we do not undertake the training to attain this knowledge, our consciousness will continue to be interrupted by the quiet intervals of our sleeping. During these quiet intervals, our souls know nothing of the outer worlds, and equally little of themselves.

At first, our dreams are only regarded as a manifestation of our sleep-life, and thus only two states are generally spoken of: that of our sleeping and of our waking. For Spiritual Science, however, dreams have an independent significance apart from the other two conditions.

In the previous chapter, descriptions were given of the alterations ensuing in our dream life while undertaking our ascent toward higher knowledge. Our dreams lose their meaningless, irregular, and disconnected characters, and form more and more into a world of law and order.

As we continue to develop, facts representing the higher realities will begin to reveal themselves. These are the secrets and riddles that lie concealed everywhere in our physical world. These effects are only seen by certain higher factors, and are not able to be penetrated if our perceptions are confined merely to our senses.

In truth, we must not regard these revelations as actual knowledge if they do not reveal themselves during our ordinary waking lives. But in time we will achieve this, as well: we will develop the ability of carrying over into our waking consciousness the conditions we created for ourselves out of our dream lives.

Accordingly, something new will be introduced into the world of our senses. Just as persons born blind who then have their eyes successfully operated on will recognize surrounding objects and be enriched by all that their eyes perceive, so too will we—having become a seer, by way of the above-mentioned manner—perceive the whole surrounding world to be filled with new qualities, things, beings, and so forth.

We will no longer need to wait for our dreams to live in other worlds. We will be able, at suitable moments, to place ourselves into the above condition for the purpose of receiving higher perceptions. It may now be said that *we have opened the eyes of our souls,* and now we behold things which habitually remained concealed from our bodily senses.

These stated conditions are only the in-between to still higher stages of knowledge. If we continue esoteric exercises, we will find in due time that these radical changes will not confine themselves only to our dream lives. These transformations will also extend to what were previously conditions of our deep dreamless sleep.

Deep Sleep

"Isolated conscious experiences will begin to interrupt the unconscious experiences within our deep sleep. Perceptions previously unknown to us will emerge from the pervading unknown through the pervading darkness of our sleep."

It is, of course, not easy to describe these perceptions, for our language is only adapted to our physical world; therefore, that which is now being expressed is only in approximate terms.

> "The belongings and beings of the higher worlds bear enough resemblance to our physical world to enable us to form some sort of conception of them. Only, we must always bear in mind that the descriptions of these supersensible worlds must, to a large extent, be in similes and symbols."

The words of our ordinary language are only partially adopted during our esoteric training; for the rest, we must learn other symbolical languages, as a natural outcome of our ascent to higher worlds. *But this does not preclude the possibility of our learning from these ordinary descriptions something concerning the higher worlds presented here.*

Somewhat of an idea may be given of the experiences which emerge from our unconsciousness during our deep sleep if we compare them to kinds of hearing—that is, of observable tones and words. While the experiences during our dreaming sleep may rightly be designated as kinds of visions, the details observed during our deep sleep may be compared to those of auditory impressions.

For the spiritual worlds, colors are higher than sounds and words. Our first perception of the higher worlds does not as yet extend to these higher colors, but only to those of the lower tones; but later on, we will ascend on to these colors and forms.

When these experiences first come to us during our deep sleep, our first task is to sense them as clearly and vividly as possible. At first this may appear difficult, for our perceptions of these experiences are exceedingly slight. Upon waking, we know very well that we had these experiences, but we are completely in the dark in regard to their nature.

The most important objective during these initial stages is to remain quiet and composed, and to never lapse into any kind of unrest or impatience. The latter is detrimental to our development under all circumstances; it will never accelerate our development, but only delay it. We must cultivate quiet and yielding receptivity for the gifts that are being presented to us. All violence must be repressed.

Should we, at any period of time, not become aware of our experiences during our sleep, we must wait patiently; for someday these moments will arise. And if we await them with both our patience and composure, they will remain our secure possessions. However, if we try to contain them by forced methods, they may be completely lost to us for a long time.

Once we have developed these perceptive abilities, our experiences during sleep present themselves to our consciousness with complete lucidity and clarity. Now our attention should be directed towards the following experiences:

There are two kinds of experiences which are clearly distinguishable. The first kind will be totally different from anything we have ever experienced. These experiences may bring us sources of great joy and enlightenment; however, they should be left alone for the time being. These experiences are the first forerunners of the higher spiritual worlds and will be discussed later.

In these other kinds of experiences, we, as attentive observers, will discover definite connections with our ordinary living world.

We now need to reflect with our ordinary intellect on our own lives and those things around us. During our daily lives, we reflect on our environments; our minds are trying to conceive and understand the connections existing between the things we are seeking to understand and the thoughts and ideas which our senses are now perceiving.

These are the ideas and concepts that our experiences during sleep are referring to. Obscure, shadowy concepts become resonant and living in ways only comparable to the tones and the words in our physical world.

They will appear to us more and more as solutions to the riddles over which we have been pondering. These are now whispered to us in tones and words out of the higher worlds. And we are now able to connect and apply them to our ordinary lives.

What was formerly accessible only through our thoughts now become actual experiences, just as substantial and alive as any of our experiences in our physical world. These things and beings in our physical world are by no means only what we appear to physically perceive. They are the expressions and influences of the spiritual worlds. What the spiritual worlds had previously concealed now echo for us out of our entire environment.

It is easy to see how these higher perceptions can prove to be blessings; but this only happens if our opened soul-senses are in perfect order, just as our ordinary bodily senses can only be used for true observations of our physical world if they are in working order. We ourselves formed these higher senses through the exercises directed by Spiritual Science.

These exercises include concentration, in which our attention is directed to certain definite ideas and concepts connected with the secrets of the universe. This is done through meditation. Meditation allows us to completely immerse ourselves in them in the correct way.

"Through this awareness and through meditation,
we can work upon our souls and develop within
them our soul-organs of perception.
By applying ourselves to these methods,
our souls grow within our bodies,
just as embryos grow within
the bodies of their mothers."

When these isolated experiences during our sleep begin, as described, the moment of our birth is approaching and we are soon to be liberated souls; for we will literally become new beings, developed by ourselves within ourselves, from seeds to fruits.

The methods spoken of above are required and must therefore be carefully and accurately maintained, for they contain the laws governing the germination and fruition of our higher selves. If we do not apply and maintain what we have learned thus far, our higher births will not take place.

Our higher soul-selves are born during our deep sleep. They are delicate organisms lacking all power of resistance and unable to appear during our physical, everyday lives. They would not prevail against the harsh and powerful processes of our lives. Here again, we must bear in mind that these experiences during our sleep are not regarded as fully valid knowledge, because we are not carrying over our awakened higher souls into our waking consciousness.

The acquisition of these abilities will enable us to perceive the spiritual worlds in their own characters, among and within the experiences of our daily lives; that is, the hidden secrets of our environments will be conveyed to our souls as tones and words.

Now, we must realize at this stage in our development that we are dealing with separate and isolated spiritual experiences. We should therefore be cautious of creating complete, whole, or even connected systems of knowledge from them. If this were the case, entirely imaginary ideas and conceptions would be mixed into our soul-worlds, and therefore our worlds might easily be constructed which have nothing to do with our real spiritual worlds.

We must continually practice self-control. The right thing for us to do is to strive for a clearer conception of our isolated real experiences, and to await the spontaneous arrivals of these new experiences which will connect themselves, of their own accord, with those already recorded.

By virtue of these powers of the spiritual worlds through which we have now found our way, and through our continued application by means of the prescribed exercises, we will experience ever-increasing extensions and expansions of consciousness during our sleep.

The unconscious intervals during our sleep-lives will grow smaller, while more and more conscious experiences will emerge out of those of which we were previously oblivious. The less our habits of thought which were developed in our physical world are allowed to play into these higher experiences, the better.

By conducting ourselves appropriately, we now approach ever closer to our attainment of the conditions that lead us on our path to this higher knowledge, in which the unconsciousness of our sleep lives is transformed into our complete consciousness. When our bodies are at rest, we live in surroundings which are just as real as those of our waking daily lives. However, these realities during our sleep are different from our physical realities surrounding our physical bodies. If we are to retain our firm footing in our physical world, we must learn not to become visionaries, and to try to connect the higher experiences of our sleep with our physical environments.

At first, however, the worlds we enter during our sleep are completely new revelations. This important stage in our development, where our consciousness is retained in our lives during our sleep, is known in Spiritual Science as the *continuity of consciousness.*

These specified conditions are regarded, at certain stages of our development, as kinds of ideals, attainable at the end of our long paths. What we first have learned is that the extensions of our consciousness occur in two soul-states: in the first state we receive only disordered dreams, and in the second we receive only our unconscious, dreamless sleep. Having reached this stage of development, we will not stop experiencing and learning during those intervals when our physical bodies are resting, or when our souls receive no impressions through the instrumentality of our senses.

– CHAPTER 8 –

THE SPLITTING OF THE HUMAN PERSONALITY DURING SPIRITUAL TRAINING

During sleep, no impressions are conveyed to our souls through our physical sense-organs. In a certain respect, our souls are outside our so-called physical bodies—and in our waking lives, they are the mediums for our sense perceptions and thoughts.

Our souls are only connected with our finer bodies (our etheric bodies and astral bodies), which are beyond the scope of our physical sense-observations. But the activities of these finer bodies do not cease during our sleep. Just as our physical bodies relate to the things and beings of our physical worlds, affecting them and being affected by them, so too do our souls live in higher worlds.

Our souls are fully active during sleep, but we know nothing of these activities so long as we have no spiritual organs of perception through which to observe what is going on around us and to see what we ourselves are doing during our sleeping. The previous chapters have shown that esoteric training assists us in the development of our spiritual sense organs. Now, as a result of these esoteric teachings, our sleeping lives are transformed in the manner described in the previous chapter, and we will be able to consciously follow everything going on around us. However, it should be noted that higher degrees of divining are required for the higher perceptions of our physical environments, as well, as indicated in the last chapter.

In the initial stages of our development, we perceived things that pertained to the other worlds without our being able to discern their connection with the objects of our daily physical environments. These characteristics, found during our sleeping or in our dreams, illustrated what is continually taking place inside us. Our souls are uninterrupted by the activities of the higher worlds, gathering from those worlds the impulses to act upon our physical bodies. Before, we were unconscious of higher worlds; but we now render ourselves conscious of them, and thereby our entire lives have become transformed.

Our soul's higher senses are guided by superior cosmic beings. And just as the lives of people who are born blind are changed through successful operations from their previous dependencies on external guides, so too are the lives of those changed through esoteric training.

We now have outgrown the principle of being guided by our masters, and must now and in the future undertake to be our own guides. The moment this occurs, we are, of course, liable to commit errors totally unknown to our ordinary consciousness. We act now from worlds which we formerly had little, if any, knowledge of. **These higher powers are directed by the universal cosmic harmonies. We must now extract from these cosmic harmonies those things which were previously done for us without our co-operation, and do them for ourselves.**

The Dangers Concerning Ascension into the Higher Worlds

There are many books dealing with matters concerning the dangers connected with ascension into the higher worlds. *Yet the fact is that these dangers only will arise when the necessary precautions are neglected.*

If we adopt and follow all the measures counseled by true esoteric science, we are assured of experiences that surpass, in power and magnitude, everything and anything our sense-bound fantasies could have imagined; and there is never any question of injury of any kind towards our health or our lives.

However, if we should neglect these necessary

precautions, we may meet with horrible forces and beings existing beyond our physical perceptions. Temptation may become great to try to control these forces for the furtherance of our own interests; and we may employ them wrongly, out of our own deficient knowledge of these higher worlds. We must realize that there are hostile powers that are present. Though it is also true that, in these circumstances, their relationship to us is ordained by higher powers, and that these relationships were altered when we consciously entered their worlds previously concealed from us—at the same time, our own existence is enhanced and the circle of our lives is enriched by these new fields of experiences.

Real danger may arise only if we, through our own impatience or arrogance, assume too early a certain independence with regard to our experiences of these higher worlds, before we are able to gain sufficient insights into the supersensible laws. However, **if we possess the qualities of modesty and humility, we may be certain that our ascent into these higher lives will be achieved without danger.**

The Spiritual Worlds Define the Facts of Our Physical World

Above all, no disharmony must ensue between these higher experiences and the events and demands of our everyday lives. Our responsibility must be entirely sought for on this earth; and anyone desiring to shirk their earthly duties by trying to escape into other worlds may be certain they will never reach their goal.

> *"What we perceive with our senses*
> *is only part of our world,*
> *and it is in the spirit worlds that*
> *the beings dwell who define the facts*
> *of our physical world."*

Therefore, **we must participate with the spirits to carry out these revelations into our physical world. We must transform the earth by implanting what we have discovered by means of these spiritual worlds. This is our task.** This is because the physical world is dependent upon the spiritual worlds; and only if we participate in the worlds in which the creative forces lie concealed, only for this reason, should we have the desire to ascend to the higher worlds.

No one approaching this esoteric training with these sentiments and these resolves need fear the slightest danger. We should not allow the prospect of these dangers to deter us from esoteric training. We should rather seek them as challenges in order to acquire the capacities which we must possess.

Development of Three Fundamental Forces of Our Souls: Willing, Feeling, and Thinking

Great changes have taken place in our finer bodies, as described above. These changes relate to certain processes in the development of the three fundamental forces of our souls, which are: our willing, our feeling, and our thinking.

Before esoteric training, these forces were subject to connections predestined by higher cosmic laws.

"Willing, feeling, and thinking are not random acts. Ideas arising in our minds are joined by feelings according to natural laws, and are followed by resolutions of our wills in equally natural sequences."

We enter a room, find it stuffy, and open the window. We are questioned, and we answer. We perceive ill-smelling objects as experiences of repulsion. These are simple connections between our thinking, feeling, and willing. When we survey human lives, we find that everything is built up on such connections. Indeed, our lives are not to be termed as normal *unless* we have such connections. These are the laws that were founded on the laws of our human nature, and that are observed among our thinking, feelings, and willing. It would be contrary to these laws if we sighted any ill-smelling object and it gave us pleasure; or if we, upon our being questioned, did not answer. Certain thoughts are conveyed to us with the assumption that they will be associated, on regular basis, with our feelings and our choices.

This connection in our finer soul-being has its counterpart in our coarser physical body. Our wills are connected, according to these laws, with our thinking and feeling. Therefore, some thoughts will inevitably evoke certain feelings and activities within our wills.

In the course of our higher development, the threads that interconnect these three fundamental forces are severed. At first, these severances occur only within our finer soul-beings; but at a still higher stage, this separation extends also to our physical bodies.

The Thought-Brain, the Feeling-Brain, and the Will-Brain

In fact, in the course of our higher spiritual development, our brain divides into three separate parts. This separation is not physically perceptible in the ordinary way, nor can it be demonstrated by the most powerful of instruments. The brain of the higher seer divides into three independently active entities: the thought-brain, the feeling-brain, and the will-brain.

Thus, our organs of thinking, feeling, and willing become individualized. Their connections from this time on are not maintained by laws inherent in and of themselves, but must be managed by our own awakened higher consciousness. These are the changes which we observe coming over us: that no connections arise from our ideas, our feelings, or our will-impulses unless we ourselves provide them.

No impulse can urge us from our thoughts to action unless we ourselves determine to give rise to this impulse.

We can, from this time on, confront—devoid of feeling—facts which, before our trainings, would have filled us with glowing love or bitter hatred; and we may remain impassive with those thoughts which, formerly, would have spurred us into action through our own accord. Now we perform our actions through the resolution of our own wills. **One of our greatest achievements is our attainment and complete mastery over the combined activities of our three soul forces; and at the same time, our responsibility for these activities is also placed entirely into our own hands.**

It is only through these transformations that we may enter consciously into our relationship with certain supersensible forces and beings, because our own soul forces are related to these certain fundamental forces of the world. These forces that are inherent in our wills may affect definite things and beings of the higher worlds, and we perceive them; but we may only do so once we are liberated from our connections with our own thinking and feeling within our own souls. The moment these connections are severed, the activities of our wills may be expressed.

The same applies to the forces of our thinking and feeling. Feelings of hatred that are sent out by other people are visible to us, yet we are able to ward them off just as ordinary persons may ward off physical blows that are aimed at them.

In the supersensible worlds, hatred becomes a visible phenomenon; but it may only be perceived insofar as we are able to project outward the forces lying within our own feelings. And what is spoken here of hatred also applies to far more important phenomena of our physical world. We may now enter conscious communication with the higher worlds, thanks to the liberation of these fundamental forces of our souls.

However, a caution: Through the separation of the forces of thinking, feeling, and willing, the possibility of a three-fold irregularity arises for anyone neglecting the injunctions given them by esoteric science. Such irregularities may occur if the connecting threads are severed before higher consciousness is sufficiently advanced. For, as a rule, the three human soul-forces are not equally advanced in their development at any given period. In one person, thinking is ahead of feeling and willing; in a second, other soul-forces have the upper hand over the others.

Yet as long as the connection among our soul-forces is maintained, as established by the higher cosmic laws, no injurious irregularities in our higher senses may occur through the predominance of one force over another.

Three Deviations that May Occur

The first deviation occurs when the predominance of our will is prevented by the effects of over-thinking and over-feeling, and lapsing into any excess. If we are not sufficiently advanced to be able to control our higher consciousness and are unable to achieve or restore harmony, our wills will continually overpower us. Our feelings and thoughts will lapse into complete powerlessness, and we will be tormented by over-mastering wills. A violent nature is the result of rushing from one unbridled action to another.

A second deviation occurs when our feelings unduly shake off proper control. If we were once inclined to revere others, we may now diverge into unlimited dependence, to the extent of losing all personal will and thought. Instead of higher knowledge, the most pitiful emptiness and weakness would become our lot. Or, in the case of excessive dominance in our feeling lives—if, for example, we were inclined towards religious devotion—we may now sink into immoral confusion.

The third deviation occurs when our thoughts predominate, allowing us to be locked up within ourselves. The world has no further importance to us, save that it provides us with objects for satisfying our boundless thirst for wisdom. No thoughts ever move us into any form of action or feeling. We appear, everywhere, as cold and unfeeling. We flee from every contact with that which would have once appealed to us in our lives, for it has lost all meaning for us.

Therefore, these are the three ways of error into which we may stray:

1. Exuberant forcefulness of our will
2. Sentimental emotionalism
3. Cold, loveless striving for wisdom

From outward observation and from the ordinary (materialistic) medical standpoint, those that have accordingly gone astray are hardly distinguishable (especially in degree) from people who are crazy or, at the very least highly imbalanced.

It is essential that all three of our fundamental soul-forces—our thinking, feeling, and willing—have undergone harmonious development before being released from their inherent connections and oriented to our awakened higher consciousness.

For once mistakes are made and one of our soul-forces falls prey to unbridled excess, our higher souls come into existence as failures. These unrestrained forces pervade our entire personalities, and for a long time there can be no question of any balance being restored.

These serious dangers do not threaten us until we have acquired the ability to include in our waking consciousness those experiences that came to us during our sleep. As long as any information received comes from the intermissions during our sleep, the lives of our senses (which are regulated by universal cosmic laws) will respond during our waking hours to any disturbed equilibrium of our souls, and will tend to and restore any imbalances. That is why it is so essential that our waking lives be regular and healthy in all respects.

> *"The more we can meet the demands made by the outer world with healthy, sound alignment with our inner worlds (bodies, minds, and spirits), the better off we are."*

On the other hand, just the opposite is true of unhealthy intrusions: for example, if, during our ordinary waking outer life, there are any destructive or hampering influences, they will affect the greater changes taking place within our inner lives.

We must use all our power and ability to seek solace in undisturbed, harmonious surroundings, while avoiding everything detrimental to this harmony. It is not so much a question of our casting off these unrests and haste in our external senses, but much more of our taking care of our thoughts, feelings, intentions, and bodily health and seeing that they are not exposed to continual fluctuations.

All this was not so easy for us to accomplish before our esoteric training; but now these higher experiences in our lives act upon our entire existence. Should anything within these higher experiences not be as they should, these irregularities continue to lie in wait for us and may, at every turn, throw us off our right path.

For these reasons, we should omit nothing which can secure for us unfailing mastery over our entire being. Genuine esoteric training gives rise to all these qualities; and as we progress, we only become more acquainted with these dangers, while simultaneously and at the right moments acquiring the full power to rout them from our fields.

– CHAPTER 9 –

THE GUARDIAN OF THE THRESHOLD

One of the most significant experiences marking our ascent into higher worlds is our meeting with the *Guardian of the Thresholds*. **There are two** *Guardians: lesser* **and** *greater*. We meet the lesser Guardian when our threads connecting our willing, feeling, and thinking within our finer astral and etheric bodies begin to loosen in the ways described in the previous chapter.

The greater Guardians are encountered when the separating of these connections extends to the physical parts of our body, the first being our brain.

An attempt will now be made to describe, in narrative form, our meetings with the lesser Guardians of the Thresholds, resulting in learning what happens when our thinking, feeling, and willing have become released from within their inherent connections. (Only some of the more important features will be indicated here.)

The Guardians proclaim their significance to some extent by the following words: Previously, there were powers invisible to us that watched over us. They saw to it that, in the course of our lives, each of our good deeds brought us rewards and each of our bad deeds was attended by unfavorable results. Thanks to these influences, our characters formed out of our own life-experiences and our own thoughts.

They were the instruments of our destiny. They ordained the measure of the joy and pain allotted to us in our incarnations, according to our conduct in our past lives. They ruled over us as the all-embracing laws of *karma*.

These powers will now partly release themselves from their constraining influences; and from this time on, we must accomplish for ourselves part of the work which they had previously performed for us.

Our destinies may have struck us many hard blows in our past, and we did not know why. Each of these blows was the consequence of the harmful deeds we had done in our former lives. We found great joy and happiness, and we took them as they came. They, too, were the fruits of our former deeds.

Our characters show our many beautiful sides, as well as many ugly flaws. We may thank ourselves for both, for they are the results of our previous experiences and thoughts. Until now, these were unknown to us.

These karmic powers witnessed all our deeds in our former lives, and all our innermost secrets, thoughts, and feelings; and they have determined, accordingly, our present selves and the present modes of our lives. Now, all the good and evil sides of our past lives will be revealed to us.

Previously, they were interwoven within our own beings; they were within us, but we could not see them. But now they release themselves from us; they detach themselves from our personalities; they assume independent forms. And we are now those very beings who shaped our bodies out of our good and bad achievements. *Our ethereal forms are woven out of our own life records.* Up to now, they had endured invisibly within us for the wisdom of our own destiny. Though concealed from us, they worked within us, so that any of those individual hideous blemishes on our forms would be blotted out.

Now that they have been brought out into view from all that was within us, all that concealed wisdom will now be taken from us, too. They now leave the work in our hands, alone. We must become perfect and glorious beings, or we will fall prey to corruption; and should this occur, we would be dragged down into dark and corrupt worlds.

If we wish to avoid this, then our own wisdom must become great enough for us to undertake the task of the concealed wisdom which has departed from us. Once we have crossed the thresholds, the *Guardians' forms become visible to us*;

and, as forms visible to us, they will never even for an instant leave our sides.

And in the future, whenever we act or think of something wrong, we will instantly perceive our guilt as a hideous, demonic distortion in its form. Only when we have made good of all our former wrongs and have purified ourselves so that all further evil is impossible for us, only then will these beings become transformed into radiant splendor. Then they too shall once again become united with us for the welfare of our future activities.

The thresholds are fashioned out of all the apprehensions that still remain within us, and out of all dread of the strength that was needed for us to take full responsibility for all our own thoughts and actions. It must be noted that if a single stone is found missing, we must remain standing as though transfixed, or else we will misstep.

We should not seek to cross these Thresholds until we feel ourselves entirely free from fear and are ready for the highest of responsibilities. Previously, we only emerged from our personalities when our deaths recalled us from our earthly lives; but even then, the forms were veiled from us.

The guardians who have watched over us and hold the power over our destinies in the intervals between our death and our new birth build in us, in accordance with our appearance, the powers and capacities thanks to our past hard labors, into our new birth lives—new, beautiful forms for our own welfare and progress. It was they, too, whose imperfections ever and again constrained the powers of our destinies to lead us back to our new incarnations upon earth.

It is only when we unconsciously transform them to complete perfection in our ever-recurring earthly lives that we can/will escape the powers of death and pass over into immortality, united with them.

Visible they stand before us today, just as they had stood invisible beside us at the hour of our deaths. When we have crossed the Thresholds, we will enter those realms to which we had previously only had access after our physical deaths. We now enter them with full knowledge; and hereafter, we wander outwardly visible upon the earth and at the same time we wander in the kingdom of death—that is, in the kingdom of our life eternal.

These guardians are indeed the Angels of Death; but at the same time, they are the bearers of our eternal higher lives. Through them, we will die with our bodies still living, to be reborn into everlasting existence. **Into these kingdoms we are now entering; we will meet beings that are supersensible and share our happiness. But we ourselves must provide our first acquaintance with these worlds, as our own creations.**

Formerly, we drew our lives from them; but now they have awakened us to a separate existence, so that we stand before them as the visible gauges of our future deeds—and perhaps, too, as our constant reproaches. What has been specified here in narrative form must not be understood by our senses as images, but as experiences of the highest possible realities befalling upon us.

The Guardians must warn us not to step further unless we feel the strength in ourselves to fulfill the demands that were made in the above reflections. However horrible the forms assumed by the Guardians, these are only the effects of our own past lives, our own characters risen out of and into our independent existences. Our awakening is brought about by the separation of our wills, thoughts, and feelings. **We will feel for the first time that we ourselves have called spiritual beings into existence, and these experiences in and of themselves are of the greatest significance.**

This preparation is aimed at enabling us to be able to endure these terrible sights without any trace of timidity and, at the moment of our meetings, to feel our strength so increased that we can undertake fully consciously the responsibility for transforming and beautifying the Guardians.

If successful, the meetings with the Guardians will result in our next physical deaths being entirely different events from the deaths that we formerly knew. We will consciously experience these deaths by laying aside our physical bodies and discarding them, much as we would have discarded garments through sudden events.

> *"Consequently, our physical death*
> *is only of special importance to those who*
> *are still living, and whose perceptions are*
> *still restricted to the world of their senses.*
> *To them, we die; but for ourselves,*
> *nothing of importance has changed*
> *in our entire environment.*
> *The entire supersensible worlds which stood*
> *open to us before our death are*
> *the same worlds that will now confront us*
> *after our death."*

The Guardians of the Threshold are also connected with other matters. We belong to our families, our nations, and our cultures. Our activities depend upon our belonging to these communities. The characters of our families, nations, and cultures also have destinies of their own.

For those who have restricted senses, these ideals remain simply general ideas. Besides separate individuals, very real families and national group souls and cultural spirits are at work in the lives of our families, people, and cultures. In a certain sense, we as separate individuals are merely the executive organs of these family group souls, cultural spirits, and so on.

The truth lies in the fact that national group souls make use of each of the individuals belonging to their nations for the carrying out of some works. These group souls do not descend into our physical realities, but rather dwell in the higher worlds; so for them to work in our physical worlds, they have to make use of our physical structures. In a higher sense, it is like architects making use of their workforce for executing the details of buildings.

Everyone receives allotted tasks from their families, nations, or cultural group souls. Now, ordinary people are by no means initiated into the higher designs of their work. They join *unconsciously* into these tasks. From the moment we meet the Guardians, we must not only know our own tasks, but we also must knowingly collaborate with those of our people and our cultures. For all delays of our prospects, it will be necessary for us to enlarge the scope of our duties.

What happens is that we add new bodies to our finer soul-bodies. Previously, we found our way through the worlds with shielded personalities; and what we had to accomplish for our communities, our nations, our cultures were directed by higher spirits who made use of our personalities.

Now, further revelations are made by the Guardians of the Thresholds that from this time on, they as spirits will withdraw their guiding hands from us. Yet as isolated personalities, we would become hardened and decline into ruin if we ourselves did not acquire the powers which are vested by our national and cultural spirits.

We could now say: *"Oh, we have entirely freed ourselves from all our lineal and cultural connections; we only want to be human beings and nothing but human beings."* To this must be replied: *"Who brought you to these freedoms? Was it not our families who placed us in the worlds where we now stand?"*

> *"Have we not our lineages, our nations, our cultures*
> *to thank for our being what and who we are?*
> *They have brought us up. And if, exalted above*
> *all prejudices, we are now one of the light-bringers*
> *and benefactors of our stocks and even*
> *our cultures, we owe it to them*
> *and our upbringings."*

Yet even when we say we are "nothing but human beings," the facts are that we have become such that we now owe to the spirit of our communities. Only we have learned what it means to be entirely cut off from our families, and our national and our cultural spirits. Everything instructed in our training has completely melted away when those threads binding our wills, thoughts, and feelings are severed. We look back on the results of all our previous training as we might on our houses crumbling away brick by brick, which we must now rebuild in a new form.

Again, these are more than mere symbolical expressions where the Guardians had pronounced their first statements; there now arises from the spots where we stand whirlwinds which extinguish all those spiritual lights that had previously illuminated the pathways of our lives. Now there is utter darkness, relieved only by the rays of lights issued from the Guardians themselves unfolding before us. And out of the darkness resounds the Guardians' further cautions: **"You must not step across our Thresholds until you have clearly realized that you yourselves light up the darkness ahead of you; and you should not take a single step forward until you are positive that you have sufficient oil in your own lamps."**

The lamps of our guides whom we have previously followed will now no longer be available to us. At these words, we must turn and glance backwards. The Guardians of the Thresholds now draw aside the veils, which up to now had been concealed deep within our lives-mysteries. Our families, nations, and cultural spirits are revealed to us in their full activities, so that we perceive clearly on one hand how we had previously been led, and no less clearly on the other hand that from these times on we will no longer enjoy their guidance. These are the second warnings received at the Thresholds from our Guardians.

Without preparation, no one could endure the sight of what has here been pointed out. These higher teachings are what make it possible for us to advance up to the Thresholds and simultaneously put ourselves in the position to find the necessary strength at the right moments. Indeed, these teachings can be so harmonious in their nature that our entries into these higher lives have relieved all and everything of any agitating or tumultuous nature. **At the Thresholds, we will now experience feelings of our blessedness, which are the keynotes of our newly awakened lives.**

These feelings of our new freedom will outweigh all other feelings and be attended by new feelings—that of our new duties and responsibilities—which will appear as something which we, in this particular stage of our lives, must take on upon ourselves.

– Chapter 10 –

LIFE AND DEATH:
THE GREATER GUARDIAN OF THE THRESHOLD

The previous chapter described how significant our meetings are with the so-called lesser Guardians of the Threshold, by virtue of the fact that we become aware of confronting supersensible beings whom we ourselves brought into existence, and whose bodies consists of the previously invisible results of our own actions, feelings, and thoughts. These unseen forces have become the cause of our destinies and our characters, and we realize how we ourselves have founded our presents from that of our pasts.

We can understand why our inner selves, now standing revealed before us, include particular inclinations and habits; and we can also recognize the origins of certain blows of fate that have befallen us. We perceive why we love some things and hate others; why some things make us happy and others unhappy. Our visible lives are explained by invisible causes. The essential facts of our lives, too—our health and illnesses, births and deaths —unveil themselves before our gaze.

We observe how, before our births, we wove the causes which led us to return to our lives. From this time on, we know that there are beings within us which are fashioned with all our imperfections in the visible world, and which can only be brought to their final perfections in this same visible world. There are no other worlds that offer these opportunities given to us to build up and complete our being.

Thanks to our insights into these supersensible worlds, we have gained better knowledge and appreciation of the true value of our visible natures than was possible before our higher teachings. These may be counted among one of our most important experiences. *Anyone not possessing these insights and who imagines these supersensible regions to be infinitely more valuable are likely to underestimate their physical world.* We, the possessors of these insights, know that without experiences in our visible physical realities, we would be totally powerless in those other invisible supersensible realities.

"Before we can live in the invisible world, we must have the necessary abilities and instruments which can only be acquired in our visible world."

Our consciousness in the invisible world is not possible without spiritual sight; but these powers of vision in the higher worlds are gradually developed through our experiences in the lower worlds. No one is born in the spiritual world with spiritual eyes without having first developed them in the physical world, any more than children could be born with physical eyes had they not already been formed within their mothers' wombs.

From these standpoints, it will also be readily understood why the Thresholds to the supersensible worlds are watched over by our Guardians. In no cases may the real insights into these regions be permitted to anyone lacking the required aptitudes. Therefore, when, at the hour of our deaths, anyone enters the other worlds while still incompetent to work in them, these higher experiences will be hidden from them until they are fit to behold them.

Once we have entered the supersensible worlds, our lives acquire quite new meaning. We now discern in the physical worlds the seeds that were ground out of the higher worlds, so that in a certain sense these higher worlds appear defective without those of the lower worlds.

Two outlooks are opened before us: the first into our pasts, and the second into our futures. Our visions extend to the past in which the physical worlds were not yet existent, for we have long ago discarded those prejudices that the supersensible worlds were developed out of our sense-worlds. We know that the former existed first, and that out of it everything physical was to be evolved. We see that we ourselves belonged to supersensible worlds before coming for the first time into our sense-worlds.

But these pristine supersensible worlds needed to pass through our sense-worlds, for without their passages any further evolution would not have been possible. The supersensible worlds could only pursue their courses when certain beings had developed the necessary aptitudes within the realms of their senses.

These beings are none other than human beings. **We owe our present existence to the imperfect stages of our spiritual existences, and are being led, even within these stages, to these perfections which will make us fit for our further work in the higher worlds.**

At this point, our outlook is directed into our futures. Higher stages of these supersensible worlds to be distinguished will contain the fruits that have matured in our physical sense-worlds. Our physical sense-worlds, as such, will be overcome by these results, and we will have the ability to live in higher worlds.

The existence of disease and death are in our physical sense-world. Our deaths merely express the fact that the original supersensible world reached a point beyond which our physical sense worlds could not progress by themselves. Thus, our new lives have evolved into battles with our universal deaths.

From the remnants of dying, our physical sense-worlds are sprouting the seeds of new ones. Therefore, we have both death and life in our world. The decaying portion of our old world is adhering to the new life-blossoming coming from it, and the process of our evolution is slowly moving forward, coming into expression most clearly in us ourselves.

These coverings that we bear are gathered from the preserved remnants of our old world, and within these sheaths the germs of our beings are maturing into that in which will

live in our future. Thus, we are twofold beings: mortals and immortals. As mortals, we are in the last stages; as immortals, we are in the first stages.

But it is only within the two-fold worlds, where we find our expressions in our sense-worlds, that we may acquire the required abilities to lead our world to immortality. **Indeed, the tasks are precisely to gather the fruits of the mortals for the immortals. And as we glance at ourselves as the result of our own work of our pasts, we cannot but say, "We have within us the elements of decaying worlds." They are at work in us, and we may only break these powers little by little, thanks to these immortal elements coming into our lives and into us.**

These are the paths leading us from our deaths to our lives. Should we speak to ourselves with full consciousness at the hour of our deaths, we would say: *"The perishing world was our task-master. We are now dying as the result of our entire past in which we are enmeshed. The soils of our mortal lives have matured the seeds for our immortal lives. We carry these with us into the other world.*

"If we had merely depended on our pasts, we could never have been born. Our past lives came to an end with our births. The time between our births and our deaths are mere expressions for the sum of values wrested from our dying pasts by our new lives; and our illnesses are nothing but the continued effects of the dying portions of our pasts."

In the above, we have found answers as to why we work our way only gradually through errors and imperfections *to that which is good and true*. Our actions, feelings, and thoughts are at first dominated by the perishing and the mortal. The latter gives rise to our sense-organs. For these reasons, these organs and all things activating them are to perish.

The imperishable will not be found in our instincts, impulses and passions, or in our organs, but only in the work produced by these organs. We must extract from the perishable everything that can be extracted, and this work alone will enable us to discard the backgrounds out of which we have

grown, and which had found their expressions in our physical sense-worlds.

Thus, the first Guardian confronts us as the counterpart of our two-fold nature in which both the perishable and imperishable are blended; and this is clearly proof of how far removed we still are from attaining these sublime luminous figures which will again dwell in the pure, spiritual worlds. To the extent to which we are entangled in our physical sense-worlds, we are exposed to our own views.

The presence of our instincts, impulses, desires, egotistical wishes, and all forms of our selfishness and so forth express themselves in these entanglements, as they do in our memberships in our cultures, our nations, and so forth; for we, with our cultures, are but steps leading us to pure humanity.

Our cultures and our nations will stand so much the higher, the more perfectly its members express the pure, ideal human types—the further they have worked their way from the physical and perishable to the supersensible and imperishable. This evolution, brought through our incarnations in ever-higher national and cultural forms, is thus the process of our liberation, so that we may finally appear in our harmonious perfection. In a similar way, our pilgrimages through ever-purer forms of our morality and religion are perfecting processes; for every one of our moral stages retains the passion for the perishable beside the seeds of our ideal futures.

The Second, Greater Guardian of the Threshold

The lower Guardian of the Threshold is joined, after a time, by the greater Guardian. This meeting with the second Guardian will again be described in narrative form:
Once we have established and recognized all the elements from which we must liberate ourselves, we are meshed by transcendent luminous beings in their magnificence. (This is difficult to describe in the words of our own human language.)

Now liberated from all physical bonds, we are confronted

by the second Guardian of the Threshold. We have released ourselves from the world of our senses. We have won the right to become inhabitants of the supersensible worlds, where our activities will now be directed. For our own sakes, we no longer require our physical bodies in their present forms.

Now we may behold them and see how sublimely they tower above all that we have made of ourselves thus far.

We have attained our present degree of perfection thanks to the abilities we were able to develop in our sense-worlds, when we were still confined to them. **But now a new era is to begin, in which we have liberated powers that must be applied to further work in the world of our senses. Previously, we had sought only our own release; but now that we have become free, we may move forward as liberators of our generations.**

Until today, we had striven as individuals; but we now seek to coordinate ourselves with the whole, so that we may bring into the supersensible worlds not only ourselves but also all things else existing in the world of our senses.

They will someday be able to unite with us, but we cannot be blessed so long as others remain unredeemed. As separate freed beings, we would not be able to enter the kingdoms of the supersensible; instead we would be forced to look down on the still-unredeemed beings in our physical world, having severed our destinies from theirs, although we and they are inseparably united.

We had inevitably descended into our sense-worlds to gather powers needed for those of the higher worlds. To separate ourselves from our fellow beings would mean that we have abused those very powers which we could not have developed without them. We could not have descended had they not done so, as well; and without them, the powers needed for our supersensible existence would fail us.

We must now share with our fellow beings these powers which we have acquired, together with them. We shall therefore be banned any entry into these higher regions so long as we have not applied all the powers that we have acquired towards the liberation of our other fellow beings.

With these powers already at our disposal, we must pause in the lower regions of these supersensible worlds. As we stand before the portal of the higher regions, and the Angels with their fiery swords stand before us guarding Paradise, they bar us any entrance as long as there are powers that went unused in our sense-worlds.

If we refuse to supply our fellow beings with these unused powers, others will come who will not refuse; and the higher supersensible worlds will receive all the fruits of the sense-worlds' labors, while we will lose from under our feet the very ground in which we were rooted. The purified worlds will develop above and beyond us, and we shall be excluded from them. We will then tread the *black paths*, while the others from who did sever their threads will tread the *white paths*.

With these words, the greater Guardian makes its presence known soon after the meeting with the first Guardian has taken place: "We know full well what is in store for us if we yield towards the temptation of any premature place in the supersensible worlds." Magnificent Splendor shines forth from the second Guardians of the Threshold; union with them looms as a far distant ideal before our soul's vision. Yet there is also the certainty that this union will not be possible until all the powers afforded by these worlds are applied to the tasks of liberation and redemption.

By fulfilling the demands of the higher light-beings, we contribute to the liberation of humanity. Should we prefer our own premature elevation into the supersensible worlds, the stream of human evolution will flow past us. After our liberation, we will not gain any new powers from the world of our senses; and if we place our work at the world's disposal, it will entail our renouncement of any further benefits for ourselves.

However, it does not necessarily follow that when we are called upon to decide, we will naturally follow this white path. This depends entirely upon whether we are so far purified at the time of our decision that there remain no traces of any self-seeking or any prospect of making our own blessedness appear desirable. *On this side, this temptation is the strongest possible, whereas on the other side no special temptation is evident. On the other side, nothing appeals to our egotism.* The gifts we receive in the higher regions of the supersensible worlds are nothing that come *to* us, but only something that flows *from* us—that is, love for the world and for our fellow beings.

Nothing that egotism desires is denied upon the black path, for the latter provides the complete gratification of our egotism, and will not fail to attract those desiring merely their own happiness, for this is indeed the appropriate path for them to follow. *No one, therefore, should expect the occultist of the white path to give any instructions for the development of their own egotistical selves. They do not take even the slightest interest in the pleasures of these individuals.*

Each may attain this for themselves, and it is not the task of the white path occultists to shorten their way; for they are only concerned with the development and liberation of all human beings and all creatures. Their instructions therefore deal only with the development of powers for collaboration in their work. Thus, they place selfless devotion and self-sacrifice before all other qualities.

They never actually refuse anyone, for even the greatest egotists can purify themselves; but no one merely seeking an advantage for themselves will ever obtain assistance from the white occultist. Anyone, therefore, who is really following the instructions of the good occultist will, upon crossing the Threshold, understand the demands of the greater Guardian. Anyone, however, who is not following their instructions can never hope to reach this Threshold.

Their instructions, if followed, produce good results or no results; for it is not part of their task to lead to egotistical pleasure and/or mere existence in the supersensible worlds. In fact, it becomes their duty to keep us away from the supersensible worlds until we may enter them with our wills for selfless collaboration.

APPENDIX TO STEINER'S LATEST EDITION (1918)

There are people who believe all our thoughts, to a certain extent, are just mere reflections of perceptions of our inner experiences. This view, however, cannot be expressed save by those who have never raised themselves to the aptitudes of experiencing with their own souls the self-sustaining lives of their own pure thoughts.

In the ordinary lives of our souls, our thoughts are almost always blended with other functions: feeling, willing, apprehension, etc. These other functions are created by our bodies. Yet our thoughts also play into them; and as they play into them, processes take place.

It is possible, through our own inner efforts, to allow the thinking parts of our inner lives to be experienced separately from everything else by involving our pure thoughts, alone, and by detaching from the scope of our soul-lives all those thoughts which are self-supporting and from which everything provided by our bodily-trained inner lives are omitted. Such thoughts reveal themselves through themselves, through what they are, as spiritual supersensible entities.

Anyone uniting themselves with such thoughts, while excluding all apprehension, all memories, and all tokens of their inner lives, know themselves to be in supersensible regions and experience themselves outside their physical bodies.

For those familiar with these processes, it becomes irrelevant to question whether our souls can live through experiences outside of our bodies in the supersensible worlds. For it would mean denying what we know by our own experiences. The above facts do not reveal themselves unless we, as individuals, first cultivate certain conditions in our souls, allowing us to become the recipients of these revelations.

Now, some people may become disbelieving when such activities are expected to be confined solely to their souls, in order that these nonessential things should be revealed to them.

They believe that they themselves were given these revelations and the included contents because they themselves prepared to receive them. They expect experiences to which they contribute nothing, and which allow them to remain passive. But what may come through such a revelation is not that of supersensible worlds but of sub-sensible worlds.

Our human waking lives do not run their course completely within our bodies. So, too, is the life of our wills, which are founded in the co-ordination with ourselves and those of cosmic beings, so that what occurs in us is simultaneously linked in the chain of cosmic occurrences. In such visionaries or mediums, as mentioned above, their beings are completely dependent on their bodies. They exclude from the lives of their souls the functions of apprehending and willing. Thus, the contents and productions of their souls are merely disclosures of their bodily lives.

Our souls acquire progressively greater independence from our bodies than those of our other functions (thinking, feeling, willing) created by our bodies. for the supersensible activities of our soul's experiences live in our pure thoughts. Supersensible experiences must be continuations of that which we have attained by our souls, when united with our own pure thoughts.

For these reasons, it is very important for us to gain knowledge of these unions in the right way; for it is from these comprehensions that the lights shine forth to bring to us correct insight into the nature of supersensible knowledge. The moment the lives of our souls descend below the levels of our clear consciousness existing in our thoughts, our souls are on the wrong paths so far as the true knowledge of the supersensible worlds is concerned. If our souls are seized by our bodily functions, what then is experienced is not the revelations of supersensible worlds but bodily revelations confined to the sub-sensible worlds.

Having penetrated to the spheres of the supersensible, our soul's experiences are of such a nature that descriptive expressions cannot be easily found. Care must be taken not to overlook the fact that, to a certain extent, in these descriptions of supersensible experiences the distances separating the actual facts from the languages used to describe them are greater than any descriptions of our physical experiences. Many expressions intended as illustrations merely indicate, in a more delicate way, the realities to which they refer.

The statement that we need personal instruction should be understood in the sense that this book itself offers personal instruction. Today, we have reached a stage in the evolution of humanity in which spiritual scientific knowledge must become far more widely distributed than it was formerly. It must be placed within the reach of every individual, to quite a different extent from in older times.

This book is only limited to the extent that further personal instruction may be necessary, beyond what is contained in this book. No doubt, there are those that may need further assistance which is of great importance for them; but it would be false to believe that there are any cardinal points not mentioned in this book.

The descriptive instructions given in this book appear as though they require the complete modifications of our entire being. Yet, when rightly read, it will be found that *these are the descriptions of the inner conditions that are required by our souls in those moments when we confront the supersensible world.*

We develop these conditions in our souls as second beings within ourselves; and our other, healthy inner beings pursue their courses in the old ways. We know how to hold these two beings apart in full consciousness, and how to make them act and react on each other in the right way. The necessity of our adopting these existing methods and their descriptions is due to the fact that all of our cognitive processes must be directed towards the supersensible, so that in those moments of such cognition, our entire beings are engaged.

It may occur for some to ask if such figurative descriptions are necessary, and if it is possible to describe these supersensible experiences as ideas without such illustrations. In reply, it must be pointed out that *in order for us to experience these supersensible realities, it is essential that we should know ourselves to be supersensible beings in supersensible worlds.*

Without these visions of our own supersensible beings fully revealed in this way, in the descriptions given of our lotus flowers (chakras) and our etheric bodies, our individual experiences of ourselves in the supersensible worlds would be as though we were placed in the sensible worlds in such a way that these things and processes around us revealed themselves, while we ourselves had no knowledge of our own bodies.

Our perception of our own supersensible forms in our soul-bodies and etheric bodies enables us to stand, conscious of ourselves, in the supersensible worlds, just as we are conscious of ourselves in the physical world through the perception of our physical bodies.

ACKNOWLEDGMENTS

I want to acknowledge:

Naomi Rose, my editor and chief, for her continual feedback and encouragement.

Clare Goodwin, my spiritual mentor and intuitive counselor, who has been ever so important in my life's journey. Clare also wrote the Foreword to this book, and helped me choose the image for the Affirmation Cards.

My late husband, Ronnie, and my children and grandchildren, for supporting me and putting up with my hours and hours in front of the computer screen, writing.

ABOUT THE AUTHOR

Born and raised in Darien, Connecticut, Eliza Joslin Kendall became familiar with the works of Steiner as a young child, when her younger sister was placed in a Steiner-based community for children with Special Needs. Since that time, she has spent her time being human, seeking different paths to get better insights into the human condition. The mother of two daughters (Cate and Allison, each in her thirties), and the grandmother of two children (Kaiden and Maddie), Eliza resides in Cape Cod, Massachusetts. Her children live in the same area.

Eliza holds a Bachelor's degree in Business Administration. She was honored by the Women's Hall of Fame for a Start-up/Small Business in 2003. She also is certified as a Transformational Life Coach and in Quantum Field Healing, and is a Grief Educator.

Over the years, a few gifted intuitives told her that a book or books were in her future. At first she was at a loss as to what this could be. Then, many years after first encountering the work of Rudolf Steiner, she picked up Steiner's book, *The Gospel of St. John*. "It resonated and made sense," Eliza recalls. "I knew, understood, and/or had experienced on so many levels much of what he was writing." This resulted in the first "Simply Steiner"© book, *The Gospel of St. John: Revisiting the Vision of Rudolf Steiner for the 21st Century*. This book which you have just read, *Knowledge of the Higher Worlds and Its Attainment*, is the second in the "Simply Steiner"© series.

Like Steiner, Eliza, too, had supersensible perceptions, which started at a very young age. While Steiner devoted his life to mostly that of the intellectual, Eliza spent hers seeking to truly understand what it is to be human, and consequently going down every path possible to see what lies ahead. "I have always felt empathy for others and a love for all things spiritual," she explains, "but also have always felt the need to understand what it is to be human!"

ABOUT THE AUTHOR

After talking to others and researching about Steiner online, Eliza found that for many of his readers, the question often starts with, "Just where do I start? How do I begin to make sense of all this information?"

She decided to simplify his writings a bit but to keep the content and its purpose intact, as well as to bring his works to 21st-century thinking. "Steiner died in his early sixties," Eliza notes. "I am writing these works in *my* early sixties. Together in one combined spirit, we share an intellectual as well as spiritual understanding of what it is to be human."

Eliza hopes that her putting forth Steiner's work in this way will inspire people from all works of life to join her Steiner-focused book clubs, use her Affirmation Cards, discuss Steiner's ideas and theories, and advance in human spiritual development in order to bring this planet to what it is meant to be: the cosmos of love.

After all, she tells us, "It starts with us!"

"The capacities by which we can gain insights into higher worlds lie dormant within each one of us."
—Rudolf Steiner

TO GO FURTHER

If you have been deepened and ignited by what you read in this book, *Knowledge of the Higher Worlds and Its Attainment*, and you would like to learn more about this and take it further into your life, my website offers various ways for you to participate.

THE SIMPLY STEINER™ BOOK SERIES

Book 1: *The Gospel of St. John: Revisiting the Vision of Rudolf Steiner for the 21st Century — Our participation in Earth's evolution as the planet of love.* Making Steiner's philosophy accessible to the modern mind and soul, it shows how to engage with the spiritual forces directing the Earth's destined transformation into the planet of Love. If you have not already read the first book in the Simply Steiner series, you can read it now by purchasing it from my website.

Book 2: You can also purchase additional copies of *Knowledge of the Higher World and Its Attainment* here, for yourself or others to ignite with Steiner's vision.

AFFIRMATION CARDS

Keyed directly to what is in Knowledge of the Higher Worlds and Its Attainment, these Affirmation Cards are available to deepen your contemplation and make your own knowledge of the higher worlds personally relevant.

  The Affirmation Card concept came to me from the spiritual realm in a dreamlike state. I was told, "Start working with index cards." So I bought some index cards, took key quotes from the book, and glued the quotations onto the cards to see what they would look like. I brought in Clare Goodwin (who wrote the Foreword to the book) to help choose a beautiful image. Now the Affirmation Cards are published and ready to be worked with. They can be used by readers of the book as well as by practitioners as a simple daily oracle / Select-from-the-Deck affirmations. (Each quote lists the corresponding chapter from the book, for easy reference.)

Book Club Discussions

The Affirmation Cards also may be used for book club discussions, in conjunction with the book, *Knowledge of the Higher Worlds and Its Attainment.*

In addition, Book-club discussion suggestions—over 140 questions for the first book in the Simply Steiner series,
The Gospel of St. John: Revisiting the Vision of Rudolf Steiner for the 21st Century—are available from my website.
Website page: https://capecodspiritualcoach.com/book-club-opportunity/

Free Book Downloads

Meditation and Concentration: Three Kinds of Clairvoyance,
by Rudolf Steiner.
In the 1960s, there was a generation inspired by peace and love—and we want to bring that energy back. How can we learn to be our best selves and work together for the good of the planet? This free ebook speaks to this.
Website page: https://capecodspiritualcoach.com/product/simply-steiner-an-introduction/

Audio Discussions and Interviews

In which I am interviewed by K. C. Armstrong, M. L. Ruscsak, and others, and share my thoughts on "Peace & Social Media Today."
Website page: https://capecodspiritualcoach.com/audio-discussions-and-interviews/

Self-Healing / Spiritual Mentorships

"There slumbers in all human beings the means to acquire the Knowledge of the Higher Worlds." —Rudolf Steiner. This may be found through Esoteric self-healing. What is Esoteric Healing? Esoteric means "hidden, meant to be found."

"Only what we experience within ourselves unlocks for us the beauties of the outer worlds. The outer worlds, with all their phenomena, are filled with divine splendors; but we must first have experienced the divine within ourselves before we can hope to discover it in our environments." —Rudolf Steiner
Website page: https://capecodspiritualcoach.com/

Intuitive / Spiritual Coaching

I offer Intuitive Readings and Spiritual Coaching, in my capacity as a Certified Transformational Life Coach and in Quantum Field Healing. I am also a Grief Educator. I welcome your inquiries.

"I have worked with Liza several times. She knows how to immediately tap into what is important in, and at, the moment. I love the fact that I am able to check in with her as needed and that she works on a sliding scale. Her intuitive readings have been spot on!"
—A.G.M., Massachusetts

"Liza is absolutely amazing! The things this woman was telling me gave me the chills. Go to her site and get a free 20-minute reading! I'll definitely be going to see her in the future for more insight." — B.C., Massachusetts

"Liza is a kind and compassionate soul with great intuitive insight and a gift for probing beyond the surface. She gently guides her clients to delve deeper to navigate their own psyches in order to discover those blocks which may be holding them back. If you are hoping to make some changes and find yourself stuck, I believe Liza will be able to help guide you in new directions and toward growth." —S.W., Texas

www.ingramcontent.com/pod-product-compliance
Lightning Source LLC
Chambersburg PA
CBHW020533080526
44583CB00013B/842